. . .for, lo, the eternal and sovereign luminous space,
where rule the unnumbered stars,
is the air we breathe in
and the air we breathe out.
And in the moment betwixt the breathing in
and the breathing out
is hidden all the mysteries
of the Infinite Garden.

—Essene Gospel of Peace

How to

A Primer on the Life-Giving Biodynamic/French Intensive Method of Organic Horticulture

*than you ever thought possible

Grow More Vegetables*

by John Jeavons

ECOLOGY ACTION of the MID-PENINSULA

on less land than you can imagine

Book and cover design by
Brenton Beck

Cover and major illustrations by
Pedro Gonzalez

FIFTH STREET DESIGN
ASSOCIATES

Marginal illustrations by
Betsy Jeavons

Typesetting by
Ann Flanagan Typography

Published by
TEN SPEED PRESS 1979
P.O. Box 7123
Berkeley, California 94707

Second Edition.
First Edition - 47,500 copies

Library of Congress Catalog
Number 79-63721
ISBN: 0-913668-98-2 (paperbound)
       0-913668-99-0 (clothbound)

Drawing of Common Ground Garden provided by Landal Institute, Sausalito, CA

Contents

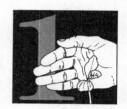

Preface

The Common Ground Garden was started in 1972 to find the agricultural techniques that would make food-raising by small farmers and gardeners more efficient. We have come to call the result "mini-farming". Mini-farms can flourish in non-agricultural areas such as mountainous regions, arid areas, and in and around urban centers. Food can be produced where people live. With knowledge and skill, output per hour can be high without the expensive machinery that is the addiction of our current agriculture. Mini-farming is available to everyone.

So far we have concentrated on the exciting possibilities presented by the biodynamic/French intensive method—does this method really produce 4 times the yield as its originator claimed? If so, does it take more water? Consume vast amounts of fertilizer and organic matter? Does it exhaust the soil? Or the people working? The only way to answer these questions was to plunge in and try it. We have mostly been working on the quantitative aspects, developing the tools and data to maximize yields within the framework of its life-giving approach. This has involved experimentation with and evaluation of plant spacings, fertilizer inputs, various watering methods and other variables. The work has always been worthwhile despite ongoing difficulties attracting strong and sustaining support. The biggest single asset to this undertaking is John Jeavons' unfailing stamina and dedication. Over and over, when we all ask, "Can it work?", he answers "How are we going to make it work?" It is becoming increasingly clear that use of the method will be an important part of the solution to starvation and malnutrition, dwindling energy supplies, unemployment, and exhaustion and loss of arable land, if the social and political barriers can be overcome.

After 7 years of testing, "the method" has produced amazing benefits and a lot of work is still to be done. YIELDS can average 4-6 times that of U.S. agriculture and range on up to 31 times. The full potential has probably not yet been reached as we are still working to bring our heavy soil to health. GRAINS and BEANS present the most challenges because they are crucial in meeting nutritional needs. Experiments include soybeans and wheat. So far our yields are equal to or double U.S. averages. WATER use is well below that of commercial agriculture per pound of food produced, and may be about one-half that used by commercial techniques per land area. ENERGY consumption, expressed in Kilocalories of input, is 1/100 that used by commercial agriculture. The human body is still more efficient than any machine we have been able to invent. Several factors contradict the popular conception of this as a labor-intensive method. Using hand tools may seem to be more work, but the yields more than compensate. At 18¢ a pound wholesale, zucchini brings us $6.00 to $12.00 per hour depending on the harvesting size. Time spent in soil preparation is more than offset later in less need for weeding, thinning, cultivation and other chores per unit of area and per unit of yield. Watering and harvesting appear to take the most time. Initial soil preparation may take up to 8 hours per 100 square foot raised bed. Thereafter the time spent decreases dramatically. A new digging tool, the U-bar, has reduced subsequent bed preparation time from 2 hours to 20 minutes. A new watering tool is also being developed which waters more quickly *and* more gently.

Use of the biodynamic/French intensive method certainly appears to make mini-farming possible. We estimate that a one-person small holding (1/2 to 1/10 acre) could grow crops bringing in a net income of up to $20,000 a year after 4 to 5 years. We hope to achieve a $10,000 income from a 1/10 acre set aside in our research garden in 1979. Crops grown will be: green onions, radishes, romaine and bibb lettuce, zucchini, patty pan squash and cucumbers. Most importantly, anyone with practice and an improved soil will be able to do it. The techniques are simple to use, as this book shows. No large capital expenses are necessary to get started. The techniques work in varied climates and soils. American farmers are "feeding the world", but mini-farming gives people the knowledge to feed themselves.

Robin Leler
Ecology Action Staff
February 4, 1979

Introduction

In September, 1971, Larry White, Director of the Nature and Science Department for the City of Palo Alto, invited Stephen Kaffka, Senior Apprentice at the Univeristy of California-Santa Cruz Student Garden, to give a four hour class on the biodynamic/French intensive method of gardening. Two years before, the City had made land available to the public for gardening and residents appeared eager to hear more about this method. Alan Chadwick had brought the method to Santa Cruz five years earlier and with love, vision and apparent magic, the master horticulturist had converted a barren slope into a Garden of Eden. Vegetables, flowers and herbs flourished everywhere. The techniques of the method were primarily available through training in a two year apprentice program at Santa Cruz and through periodic classes given by Alan Chadwick or Stephen Kaffka. However, neither detailed public classes nor vegetable yield research were being conducted regularly at Santa Cruz or in Palo Alto.

In January, 1972, Ecology Action's Board of Directors approved a biodynamic/French intensive method research and education project. The purposes of the Ecology Action project were

- to teach regular classes

- to collect data on the reportedly fourfold yields produced by the environmentally sound horticultural method

- to make land available for gardening to additional mid-peninsula residents

- to publish information on the method's techniques.

In May, after a five month search for land, the Syntex corporation offered 3-3/4 acres of their grounds in the Stanford Industrial Park at no cost and all the water needed for the project. Frank Koch, Syntex Public Affairs Director, told Dr. Alejandro Zaffaroni of the Alza Corporation about the project and Dr. Zaffaroni subsequently contributed the first money to the project, $5,000 without which we never could have begun. Commitment by Frank Koch, Don Keppy, Chuck and Dian Missar, Ruth Edwards, Ibby Bagley, numerous individuals, several corporations and the Point Foundation enabled the project to continue.

Alan Chadwick soon visited the garden site and gave us basic advice on how to proceed. We then attended a series of lectures given by Mr. Chadwick in Saratoga, California. Using the classes taught by Alan Chadwick and Stephen Kaffka as a base, we began teaching our own classes in the spring of 1972.

Further study and experience in the garden have made it possible to increase the original class to a five week series which is continually "recycled". The series of classes led to the development of information sheets on topics such as vegetable spacings and composting techniques. Many people asked for a book which contains all the information we have gathered. Those who have been unable to attend our Saturday classes or have friends who live outside the area have been especially insistent. This book is the result. Robin Leler, Betsy Jeavons, Tom Walker, Craig Cook, Rip King, Bill Spencer, Claudette Paige, Kevin Raftery, Marion McClure, Phyllis Anderson, Wayne Miller, members of Ecology Action and friends, have all made important contributions to its content and spirit.

I assume responsibility for any inaccuracies which may have been included—they are mine and not Alan Chadwick's or Stephen Kaffka's. The book is not intended to be an exhaustive work on the subject, but rather one of simple completeness. We, ourselves, are only at a beginning to intermediate stage of knowledge. Its purpose is to "turn on" as many people as possible to a beautiful, dynamically alive method of horticulture and life. I hope that the great interest this book is stimulating will eventually encourage Alan to write an extensive work on the many sophisticated techniques which only he knows well.

Our initial research seems to indicate that the method can produce an average of 4 times more vegetables per acre[1] than the amount grown by farmers using mechanized and chemical agricultural techniques. The method also appears to use 1/8 the water[2] and purchased nitrogen fertilizer, and 1/100[3] the energy consumed by commercial agriculture, per pound of vegetable grown. The flavor of the vegetables is usually excellent and

1,2. Based on data collected through 1978.

3. November 2, 1973, letter from Richard Merrill, Director of the New Alchemy Institute-West, Pescadero, California. Data were collected and evaluated by Mr. Merrill and Michael J.

there are indications that their nutritive value can be higher. The method is exciting to me because each of us becomes important again as we find our place *in relation* to nature.

With "the method" we help provide for the needs of the plants instead of trying to dominate them. When we provide for these real needs, the plants bounteously provide more food. One person annually consumes in food the energy equivalent (in calories or British Thermal Units) of 32.6 gallons of gasoline.[4] In contrast, the best economy car available will use that much gas in a month or two or ordinary driving. Imagine the fuel consumed by a tractor or industrial machine each year! People are not only beautiful, they are very capable and efficient! At this point we believe "the method" can even produce more net income per acre than commercial agriculture. In striving for quality, a person will be able to provide a diet and income more than sufficient for his or her needs. The effort will produce a human renaissance and a cornucopia of food for all.

John Jeavons
February 4, 1979
Palo Alto, California

Perelman, Assistant Professor of Economics, California State University at Chico. The data are for a growing area with a proper humus content after a 5 year development period. The data are a qualitative projection and have been assembled during a three year period of tests performed on root and leaf crops (except brassicas) grown by hand cultivation in the Santa Barbara area with its 9 month growing season. (The 1/100 figure does not include the energy required to get the soil system to the point noted above and does not include unproductive plots which constituted 10% of the area under cultivation.)

4. Michael Perelman, "Efficiency in Agriculture: The Economics of Energy," *Radical Agriculture*, Edited by Richard Merrill, Harper and Row, New York, 1976, p. 86.

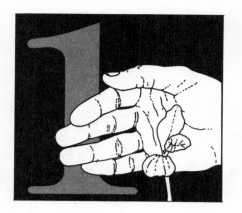

History and Philosophy

The biodynamic/French intensive method of horticulture is a quiet, vitally alive art of organic gardening which relinks man with the whole universe around him—a universe in which each of us is an interwoven part of the whole. People find their place by relating and cooperating in harmony with the sun, air, rain, soil, moon, insects, plants and animals rather than by attempting to dominate them. All these elements will teach us their lessons and do the gardening for us if we will only watch and listen. We each become gentle shepherds providing the conditions for plant growth.

The biodynamic/French intensive method is a combination of two forms of horticulture begun in Europe during the late 1800's and early 1900's. French intensive techniques were developed in the 1890's outside Paris on two acres of land. Crops were grown on an eighteen inch depth of horse manure, a fertilizer which was readily available. The crops were grown so close to each other that when the plants were mature their leaves would barely touch. The close spacing provided a *mini-climate* and a *living mulch* which reduced weed growth and helped hold moisture in the soil. During the winter glass jars were placed over seedlings to give them an early start. The gardeners grew nine crops each year and even grew melon plants during the winter.

The biodynamic techniques were developed by Rudolf Steiner, an Austrian genius, philosopher and educator in the early 1920's. Noting a decline in the nutritive value and yields of crops in Europe, Steiner traced the cause to the use of the newly introduced synthetic, chemical fertilizers and pesticides. An increase was also noticed in the number of crops affected by disease and insect problems. These fertilizers were not complete and vital meals for the plants, but single, physical nutrients

Winter lettuce growing in 1890's Cloche (Bell-Glass). Standard diameter 16 3/4 inches.

in a salt form. Initially, only nitrogen fertilizers were used to stimulate growth. Later phosphorous and potash were added to strengthen the plants and to minimize disease and insect problems. Eventually, trace minerals were added to the chemical larder to round out the plants' diet. After breaking down nutrients into their component parts for plant food, people found it necessary to recombine them in mixtures approximating a balanced diet. This attempt might have been more successful if the fertilizers had not caused chemical changes in the soil which eventually destroyed its structure, killed its beneficial microbiotic life and ruined its ability to make nutriments in the air and soil available to plants.

Rudolf Steiner returned to the more gentle, diverse and balanced diets of organic fertilizers as a cure for the ills brought on by synthetic, chemical fertilization. He stressed the holistic growing environment of plants: their rate of growth, the synergistic balance of their environments and nutriments, their proximity with other plants and their various *companion* relationships. He initiated a movement to scientifically explore the relationship which plants have with each other. From centuries of farmer experience and from tests, it has been determined that flowers, herbs and weeds can minimize insect attacks on plants. Many plants benefit one another. Strawberries and green beans produce better when grown together. In contrast, onions stunt the growth of green beans. Tomatoes are narcissists—they prefer to be grown alone in compost made from tomato plants.

The biodynamic method brought back raised planting beds. Two thousand years ago, the Greeks noticed that plant life thrives in landslides. The loose soil allows air, moisture,

Artificial fertilization

Natural fertilization

French gardeners at lettuce beds —early 1900's.

(Left) Biodynamic/French intensive raised bed (Right) traditional rows.

Row plants are more susceptible to soil compaction.

warmth, nutriments[5] and roots to properly penetrate the soil. The curved surface area between the two edges of the landslide bed provides more surface area for the penetration and interaction of the natural elements than a flat surface. The simulated landslides or raised beds used by biodynamic gardeners are usually 3 to 6 feet wide and of varying lengths. In contrast, the planting rows usually made by gardeners and farmers today are only a few inches wide with wide spaces in between. The plants have difficulty growing in these rows due to the *extreme* penetration of air and the greater fluctuations in temperature and moisture content. During irrigation, water floods the rows, immerses the roots in water and washes soil away from the rows and upper roots. Consequently, much of the beneficial microbiotic life in the roots and soil, which is so essential to disease prevention and to the transformation of nutriments into forms the plants can use, is exterminated and may even be replaced by harmful organisms. (About three-quarters of the beneficial microbiotic life inhabits the upper six inches of the soil.) After the water penetrates the soil, the upper layers dry out. The rows are then more subject to wide temperature fluctuations and air penetration. Finally, to cultivate and harvest, people and machines trundle down the troughs between the rows, compacting the soil and the roots which eat, drink and breathe—a difficult task with someone or something standing on the equivalent of your mouth and nose!

These difficulties are also often experienced at the *edges* of biodynamic/French intensive raised beds prepared in clay soils during the first few seasons. Until the soil texture becomes friable, it is necessary to level the top of the raised bed to minimize erosion (see chapter on Bed Preparation) and the soil on the sides of the beds is too tight for easy planting. Increased exposure to the elements occurs on the sides and the tighter soil of the paths is nearby. The plants along the sides usually do not grow as vigorously as those further inside the bed. When raised beds are prepared in friable soil, the opposite is true. The top of the bed is curved (see drawing at top of page) and the soil is loose enough for plants to thrive along the sides. The mini-climate effect is added to the edges of the beds and the water that runs off the inside of the bed provides the extra moisture which is needed.

5. A nutriment is "something that nourishes or promotes growth and repairs the natural wastage of organic life." It differs from a nutrient which is merely "a nourishing substance or ingredient."

During the time between the 1920's and the 1960's, Alan Chadwick, an Englishman, combined the biodynamic techniques and the French intensive techniques into the biodynamic /French intensive method. The United States was first exposed to the combination when Mr. Chadwick brought the method to the four acre organic Student Garden at the University of California-Santa Cruz campus in the 1960's. Alan Chadwick, a horticultural genius, has been gardening for half a century and is also an avid dramatist and artist. He studied under Rudolf Steiner, the French gardeners, George Bernard Shaw, and worked as a Gardener for the State of South Africa. The site he developed at Santa Cruz was on the side of a hill with a poor clayey soil. Not even "weeds" grew there—except poison oak which was removed with pick-axes. By hand, Alan Chadwick and his apprentices created soil. From this soil and vision, a beautiful, wonderous and real Garden of Eden was brought into existence. The original barren soil was made *fertile* through extensive use of compost, with its life-giving humus. The humus produced a healthy soil that grew healthy plants less susceptible to disease and insect attacks. The many nuances of the biodynamic/French intensive method—such as transplanting seedlings into a better soil each time a plant is moved and sowing by the phases of the moon— were also used. The result was beautiful flowers with exquisite fragrances and tasty vegetables of high quality. As an added bonus for all the tender loving care they received, the vegetable plants produced yields four times greater than those produced by commercial agriculture.

Lush growing beds at Common Ground make optimal use of garden space.

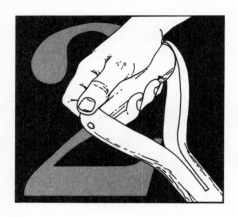

Bed Preparation

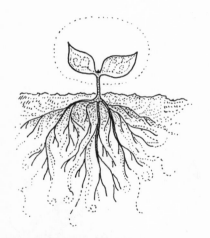

Proper soil structure and nutriments allow uninterrupted and healthy plant growth.

The preparation of the raised bed is the most important step in biodynamic/French intensive gardening. The proper texture and nutriments allow uninterrupted and healthy plant growth. Loose soil with good nutriments enables roots to penetrate the soil easily and a steady stream of nutriments flows into the stem and leaves. How different from the usual situation when a plant is transferred from a flat with loose soil and the proper nutriments into a hastily prepared backyard plot or a chemically stimulated field. Not only does the plant suffer from the shock of being uprooted, it is also placed in an environment where it is more difficult to grow. The growth is interrupted, the roots have difficulty getting through the soil and obtaining food, and the plant develops more carbohydrates and less protein than usual. Insects prefer the carbohydrates. The plant becomes more susceptible to insect attack and ultimately to disease. A debilitating cycle has begun which often ends in the use of pesticides that kill soil life and make the plant less healthy. More fertilizers are then used in an attempt to boost the health of the plants. Instead, the fertilizers kill more soil life, deplete the texture of the soil further, and bring into being even sicker plants that attract more insects and need more toxic "medicines" in the form of pesticides and additional fertilizers. There are well documented reports on a wide variety of commercial pesticides, which kill beneficial invertebrate predators while controlling pest populations. These pesticides exterminate earthworms and other invertebrates that are needed to maintain soil fertility. The pesticides also destroy microorganisms that provide symbiotic relationships between the soil and plant root systems. Why not strive for good health in the first place!

Unless you are lucky enough to have loose soil, preparing and planting a raised bed takes a lot of work—as much as 6 to 12 hours for a 100 square foot bed 5 feet by 20 feet the first time. After the first crop, however, only 4 to 6 hours should be required because the soil will have better texture. Once the beds are planted, only about 5-10 minutes a day are required to maintain a 100 square foot area—an area large enough to provide one person with vegetables 12 months a year in a community with a 4-6 month growing season.[6] Even less time and area are required in an area with an 8-12 month growing season. Beginning gardeners may require a 200 square foot area for the same yield, but we recommend a new gardener only use 100 square feet and allow his or her improving skills and soil to gradually produce more food. It is much easier.

The square feet required to provide the vegetable supply for one person are approximate since the exact amount varies depending on whether the individual likes corn (which takes up a lot of space per pound of edible vegetable grown), or a lot of carrots, beets, potatoes, and tomatoes (which require much less area per pound of food produced). Using the tables in the Planning chapter (based on yields produced by the method for all vegetable crops), the homeowner or farmer can determine the actual amount of area that should be allowed for each crop.

An Instruction Chart for the first preparation of a 100 square foot bed in a heavy clay, very sandy, or good soil is given below. A chart for the repreparation of a bed each season is also given. After the soil has been initially prepared you will find the biodynamic/French intensive method requires less work than the gardening technique you presently use. In addition, you will receive good tasting vegetables and an average of four times as many vegetables to eat! Or, if you wish to raise only the same amount of food as last year, 1/4 the area will have to be dug, weeded and watered.

6. The area during the growing seasons involved can yield 300 pounds of vegetables (and more) even when a diversity of crops is grown. The average person in the United States consumes about 322 pounds of vegetables and soft fruits annually.

INITIAL PREPARATION

Perform a Soil Test (see soil test section in the section on Fertilization)

1. Soak area to be dug for 2 hours with a sprinkler (for hard, dry clays)

2. Let soil dry out partially for 2 days

3. Loosen soil 12 inches deep with spading fork and remove weeds: 1-2 hours

4. Let soil rest for 1 day. If your soil has particularly large clods you can wait several extra days, and the action of the warm sun, cool nights, wind and water will help break the clods down. Let nature help do the work! Water the bed lightly each day to aid the process. Sand may be added to a bed with clayey soil at this time to improve

its texture. Normally not more than a 1 inch layer of sand (8 cubic feet) should be added, as more may allow the water-soluble fertilizers to percolate down too rapidly. Mix the sand thoroughly into the upper 12 inches with a spading fork: 1 hour.

5. Add a 3 inch layer (1 cubic yard or 27 cubic feet per 100 square feet) of compost (preferably) or aged manure[7] to soil with poor (very sandy or very clayey) texture. Add only a 1 inch layer (8 cubic feet) in good soil—to the surface of the bed. Mix thoroughly into the upper 12 inches with a spading fork: 1-2 hours.

6. Let soil rest for 1 day.

7. "Double-dig" the soil with a flat spade and spading fork. Be sure to use a digging board to avoid unnecessary compaction of the soil. (See pages 10 to 13 for "double-digging" instructions.): 2-4 hours.

8. Level and shape bed: 1 hour

9. Let soil rest for 1 day if working with a heavy soil.

10. Add organic nitrogen, phosphorus, potash, calcium and trace mineral fertilizers (such as blood, fish, hoof and horn, cottonseed, bone and kelp meals, wood ash and eggshells) indicated by the soil test to surface of bed after leveling and shaping bed. pH modifiers (such as leaf/pine needle compost to make the soil less alkaline, or lime to make the soil less acid) indicated as desirable by a soil test should also be included at the time. Sift in fertilizers and pH modifiers 2-3 inches deep with spading fork. Reshape bed if needed. Tamp bed down with the digging board by placing the board on various sections of the bed and then standing on the board. This removes excess air from the upper few inches of the bed: 1-2 hours

11. Plant or transplant: 1-2 hours

TOTAL: 6-14 hours

7. 2 year old steer or cow manure, or 2 year old horse manure containing a lot of sawdust or 2 *month* old horse or chicken manure not containing much sawdust.

PREPARATION FOR REPLANTING

1. "Double-dig" the soil after adding a 1 inch layer (8 cubic feet) of compost to the top of the bed: 2-3 hours

2. Shape bed: 1/2 hour

3. Let soil rest for one day if soil is still heavy

4. Add any fertilizers and pH modifiers indicated by soil test plus 1/4 inch layer (2 cubic feet) aged manure to the surface after shaping the bed. Sift in materials 2-3 inches deep with spading fork: 1/2 hours

5. Plant or transplant: 1-2 hours

TOTAL: 4-6 hours

The goal of "double-digging" is to loosen the soil to a depth of 24 inches below the surface of the soil. The first year you may only be able to reach 15 to 18 inches with reasonable effort.

The proper tools will make the work easier and more productive.

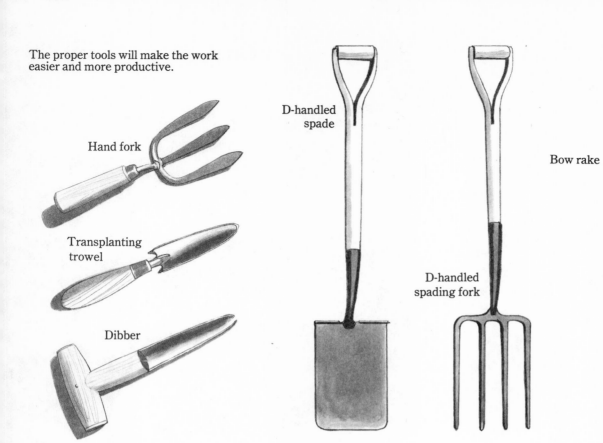

Hand fork

Transplanting trowel

Dibber

D-handled spade

D-handled spading fork

Bow rake

Be satisfied with this result. Do not strain. More important than perfection the first day or year or two is going in the right direction. Nature, the loose soil, worms, and the plant roots will further loosen the soil with each crop so that each year digging will be easier and depth will increase 3 to 6 inches. This is easier on you and your tools!

For all around ease, D-handled flat spades and D-handled spading forks of good temper are usually used for bed preparation. (Poor tools will wear out rapidly while the garden area is being prepared.) D-handles allow the gardener to stand straight with the tool directly in front of him. A long handled tool must frequently be held to the side of the gardener. This position does not allow for a simple, direct posture and leverage. When digging for long periods of time, the use of a D-handled tool is, therefore, less tiring for many people (though it will probably take the digging of 3 beds to get used to!). However, people with back problems may need long handled tools. Good strong shoes, or preferably boots, with good soles should be worn while digging.

The flat spade has a particular advantage in that it digs equally deep all along its edge rather than along a pointed "V" pattern. This is especially important in the double-dig when all points in the bed should be dug to an equal depth. The blade of the flat spade also goes into the soil at less of an angle and without the curve of the usual shovel. This means the sides of the bed can be dug perpendicular or even diagonally outward into the path, a plus for root penetration and water flow.

Note the difference in side views of shovels

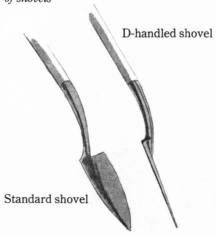

D-handled shovel

Standard shovel

The Double-dig Process

Step by Step

1.

2.

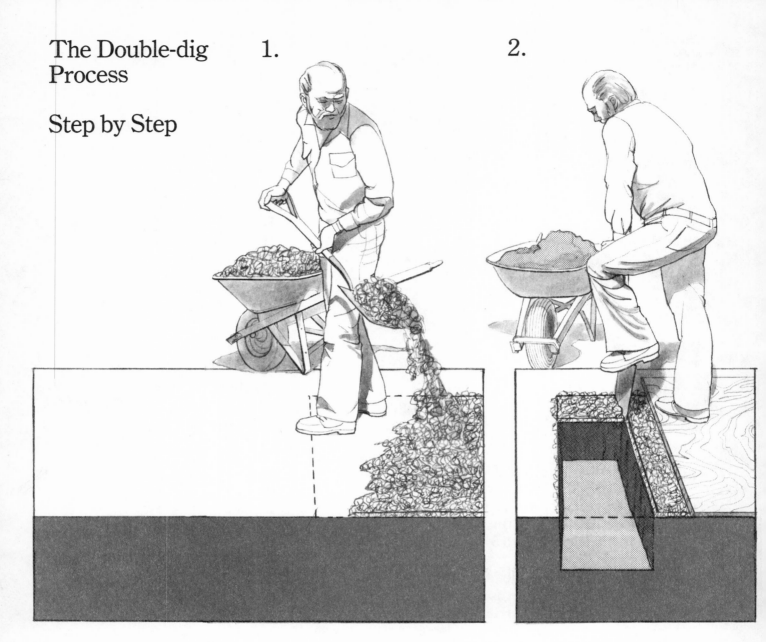

1. Spread a layer of compost over entire area to be dug.

2. Using a spade, remove soil from a trench 1 foot deep and 1 foot wide across the width of the bed. Place the soil at far end of bed.

Sides of bed should be dug outward into path.

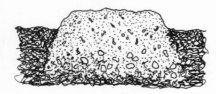

Digging should only be performed when the soil is evenly moist. It is easier and better for the soil. Digging a hard, dry soil pulverizes the structure and it is difficult to penetrate. Wet soil is heavy and easily compacted. Compaction destroys a friable structure and minimizes aeration. These conditions kill microbiotic life. The main reason for drying out periods after watering the soil is so the proper moisture level can be reached and to make digging enjoyable and beneficial. Soil is too dry for digging when it is loose and will not hold its shape after being squeezed in the palm of your hand (in the case of sands or loams) or when it is hard, dry and cannot easily be penetrated by a spade (in the case of clays). Soil is too wet when it sticks to the spade as you dig.

"Double-digging" is the term used for the process of preparing the soil two spades deep (about 24 inches). To begin, mark out a bed 3-5 feet wide and at least 3 feet long. Most people prefer a bed 5, 10 or 20 feet long but the maximum is up

3. **4.** **5.**

to you. To double-dig, remove the soil from a trench 1 foot deep and 1 foot wide across the width of one end of the bed. Use a 5/8 inch thick plywood board, 2-3 feet long by 3-5 feet wide, to stand on. Place it on top of the compost layer you spread over the bed and advance it along the bed 1 foot at a time as you prepare to dig each new trench. Move the soil from the first trench to the path in back of the last trench you intend to dig at the far end of your bed. You can move the soil by hand with the shovel or by wheelbarrow. (When you are through double-digging, you will need the soil from the first trench to fill in the open trench which remains at the back of the bed.) Next, standing in the trench, dig down another 12 inches (if possible) with a spading fork a few inches at a time if the soil is tight. Leave the fork as deep as it has penetrated and loosen the subsoil layer by pushing the fork handle down and levering the tines through soil. If the soil is not loose enough for this process, lift the chunk of soil out of the trench on the fork tines. Then throw the chunk slightly upward

3. *In good soil:* While standing in trench, loosen soil an additional 12 inches with a spade by digging into its full depth, lifting soil out on spade pan and then tipping pan downward so that the loosened, aerated soil slides back into trench. Mix up soil layers as little as possible.

4. *Alternate for moderately compacted soil:* loosen soil an additional 12 inches with a spading fork by digging tool into its full depth and then pushing tool handle downward so fork tines will lever through soil, loosening and aerating it.

5. Dig out upper part of second trench 1 foot deep and 1 foot wide. Throw each spadeful of soil forward, mix up soil layers as little as possible.

6a.   **6b.**   **7.**

6a. *Alternate for compacted soil:* while standing in trench, loosen soil an additional 12 inches with a spading fork by digging in the tool to its full depth, and lifting out a tight soil section on the fork pan.

6b. Then, by moving your arms upward in a small jerk, cause the soil to break apart as it falls downward, hits the fork tines, and falls into the hole below.

7. Spade the soil at the end of the bed (which came from the upper part of the first trench) into the open upper part of the last trench.

and allow it to fall back down on the tines so it will break apart. If this does not work, use the points of the fork tines to break the soil apart. Work from one end of the trench to the other in this manner.

Next, dig a trench behind the first one throwing each spadeful of soil forward. Sometimes you will have to go over a trench a second or third time to remove all the soil and obtain the proper trench size. Repeat the subsoil loosening process in the second trench. Dig a third trench and so on until the entire bed has been double-dug. At the end, spade the soil carried to the back of the bed into the open last trench.

When you are throwing the soil forward from one trench into another, notice two things. First, the compost layer you have added to the surface of the bed before beginning to dig slides six to nine inches down into the trench along the small mound of soil or landslide. This approximates the way nature adds leaves, flower bodies and other decaying vegetation to the

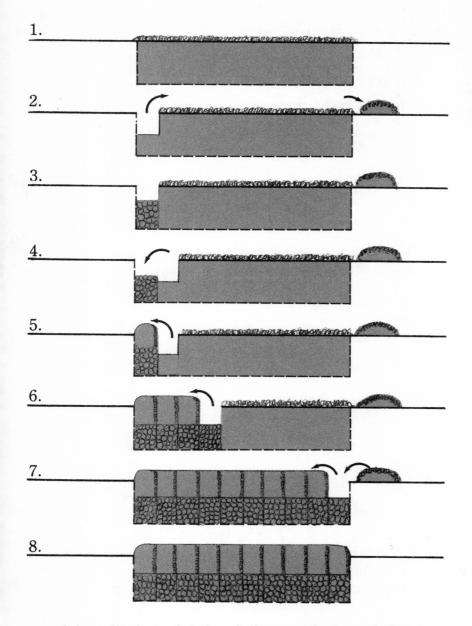

THE DOUBLE-DIG

1. Spread a layer of compost over entire area to be dug.

2. Remove soil from upper part of first trench and place at far end of bed.

3. Loosen soil an additional 12 inches.

4. Dig out upper part of second trench and throw forward into upper, open part of first trench.

5. Loosen lower part of second trench.

6. Continue "double-digging" process (repeating steps 4 and 5) for remaining trenches.

7. Place soil in mound at end of bed into open, upper part of last trench.

8. The completed "double-dig" bed.

Note that topsoil is moved forward and loosened trench by trench, while subsoil is loosened without being moved or turned.

top of the soil where they break down and where their essences can percolate into the soil. Second, the *upper* layer should not be turned over during the double-dig and succeeding double-digs. Most of the microbiotic life lives in the upper 6 inches of the soil. Also, the natural layering of the soil which is caused by gravity, water and other natural forces is less disturbed when the soil is not generally mixed, even though the soil is loosened up and mixed a little. Thus, there is a balance between nature's natural stratification and man's shepherding landslide loosening.

Once the bed is prepared, you will find great advantages in its width. The distance between the tips of your fingers and nose is about 3 feet when your arm is extended. This means a 3-5 foot wide bed can be fertilized, planted, weeded and harvested from each side with relative ease. Insects can be controlled in the same way without walking on the beds. A 3-5 foot width also allows a good mini-climate to develop. You may wish to use a narrower bed 1 1/2 to 2 1/2 feet wide for plants which

SELECTED VEGETABLE ROOT SYSTEMS SHOWN IN SCALE

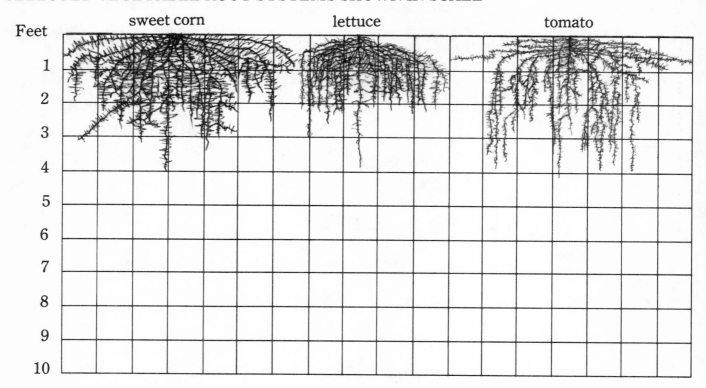

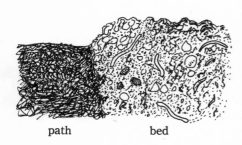

Soil in path is subject to compaction, soil in bed remains loose.

The loosened soil of the planting bed makes weeding easier. The entire weed root usually comes out intact.

are supported by stakes, such as tomatoes, pole beans and pole peas. Normally, one does not step on the plant beds once they have been prepared. To do so compacts the soil and makes it more difficult for the plants to grow. If the bed must be walked on, use the double-digging board. This will displace your weight over a large area and minimize the damage. Plants obtain much of their water and nutriment through the contact of their root hairs with the soil. If the plants lose these root hairs, less water and nutriment is taken in. Many plants lose root hairs while pushing through tight soil, so keep your soil loose!

When weeding, note that the entire weed root usually comes up out of loosened raised bed soil. This is a welcome change to the weeding process—and, if you get all the root, you will not have to weed as often. Also, you do not need to cultivate the soil of raised beds as much. The *living mulch* shade cover provided by the mature plants helps to keep the soil surface loose. If the soil compacts between the young plants before the mini-climate takes effect, you should cultivate.

Once this beautifully alive bed is prepared, it should be kept evenly moist until and after planting so the microbiotic life and plants will stay alive. It should be planted as soon as is convenient, so the plants can take advantage of the new surge of life made possible by the bringing together of the soil, compost, air, water, sun and fertilizers.

A good growing bed will be 4 to 12 inches higher than the original surface of the soil. A good soil contains 50% air space. (In fact, adequate air is one of the missing ingredients in most

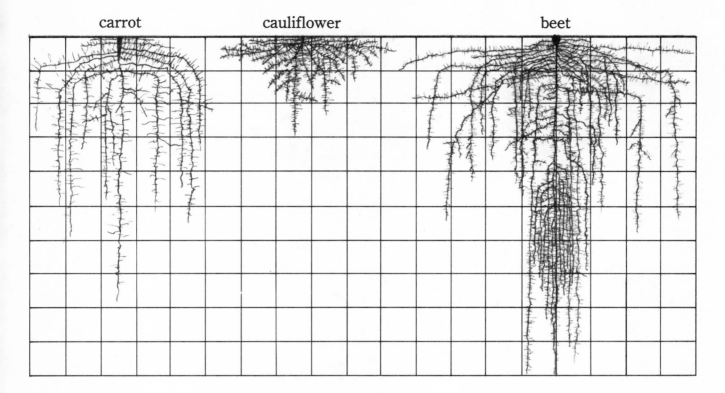

carrot　　　　　　cauliflower　　　　　　beet

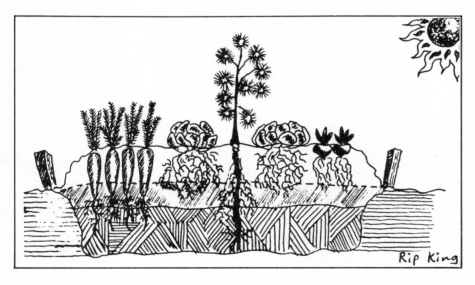

Rip King

The biodynamic/French intensive method raised bed. A balance between nature's natural stratification and man's shepherding landslide loosening.

soil preparation processes.) Thus, the prepared depth will be as much as 36 inches in clayey soil. A sandy soil will probably not raise as high as a clayey soil at first. Whenever you re-dig a bed (after each crop or season), the 24-inch depth of the bed should be measured from the top of the bed, rather than from the path surface. We currently reprepare the soil after each crop. Some people prefer to do this only once each year. As your soil improves, and the large clods disappear, your bed may not raise as high as initially. Do not worry about this. It is just a sign that you and your soil are being successful. The goal of double-digging is not in the height of the bed, but in the looseness and structure of the soil.

Fertilization

Taking a soil sampling.

I f you can, test your soil for nitrogen, phosphorous, potash and pH (the acidity or alkalinity level of your soil) before choosing your fertilizers. The best testing kit to use is the *La Motte kit*[7a]. It uses large amounts of test liquids to smaller amounts of soil and has large test tubes. All this insures a good "wetting" of the soil being tested and reduces the error margin. We have experienced significant errors sometimes with smaller kits.

To take a soil sample from your yard, use a trowel and take soil from a level 2-6 inches below the surface. Do not handle the soil with your hands. Take samples from 3 to 4 representative areas and mix them together. Make sure organic matter, such as roots are not included in the samples. Also, do not sample for 2 weeks after any fertilizers, manure or compost has been added to the area. The samples should normally be taken at the end of a season and just before the next one. You will need 4 heaping tablespoons of soil total. Mix the samples together well before beginning the tests. Remember that soil tests can save you a lot of money, since they will often indicate that the soil contains some of the nutriment needed for good plant growth. Let the samples dry in a small paper bag in indirect sunlight— *not* in the sun or an oven. You are now ready to begin the test. Use the easy to understand instructions included with the kit. Record your results on a photocopy of the chart on the following page.

Once you have completed the test, use the information on the following pages to determine a fertilization program.

7a. La Motte Chemical Products, Box 329, Chestertown, Maryland 21620

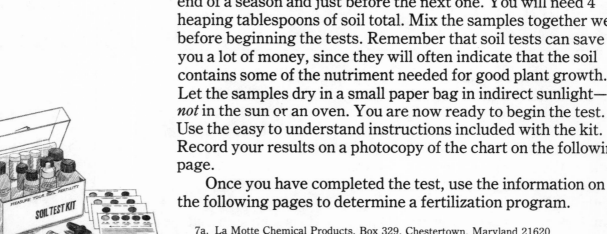

SOIL TEST

Date Performed: _____

Performed by: _____

Test	Results	Recommendations
Nitrogen		
Phosphorus		
Potash		
pH - (6.5 or slightly acid is optimum)		
Remarks (including texture)		

NITROGEN (N), PHOSPHOROUS (P) AND POTASH (K)

Pounds of fertilizer to add per 100 square feet. Pounds of *pure* nutriment added given in parentheses.

Test Rating	Nitrogen (N)	Phosphorous (P)	Potash (K)
Very High[8]	**(.1)** .75 lb. blood meal or 1 lb. fish meal or 2 lbs. cottonseed meal or .75 lb. hoof and horn	**(.2)** 1 lb. bone or 2 lb. phosphate rock or soft phosphate	**(.15)** 1 lb. kelp meal[9] or 2 lb. greensand or 3 lb. crushed granite
High[8]	**(.2)** 1.5 lbs. blood meal or 2 lbs. fish meal or 4 lbs. cottonseed meal or 1.5 lbs. hoof and horn meal	**(.3)** 1.5 lb. bone or 3 lbs. phosphate rock	**(.2)** 1 lb. kelp plus .66 lb. greensand or 1 lb. granite; or 2.66 lb. greensand; or 4 lbs. granite
Medium High	**(.25)** 2 lbs. blood meal or 2.5 lbs. fish meal or 5 lbs. cottonseed meal or 2 lbs. hoof and horn meal	**(.35)** 1.75 lbs. bone or 3.5 lbs. phosphate rock	**(.25)** 1 lb. kelp plus 1.33 lb. greensand or 2 lb. granite; or 3.33 lbs. greensand; or 5 lbs. granite
Medium	**(.3)** 2.25 lbs. blood meal or 3 lbs. fish meal or 6 lbs. cottonseed meal or 2.25 lbs. hoof and horn meal	**(.4)** 2 lbs. bone or 4 lbs. phosphate rock	**(.3)** 1 lb. kelp plus 2 lbs. greensand or 3 lbs. granite; or 4 lbs. greensand; or 6 lbs. granite
Medium Low	**(.35)** 2.75 lbs. blood meal or 3.5 lbs. fish meal or 7 lbs. cottonseed meal or 2.75 lbs. hoof and horn meal	**(.45)** 2.25 lbs. bone or 4.5 lbs. phosphate rock	**(.35)** 1 lb. kelp plus 2.66 lbs. greensand or 4 lbs. granite; or 4.66 lbs. greensand; or 7 lbs. granite
Low	**(.4)** 3 lbs. blood meal or 4 lbs. fish meal or 8 lbs. cottonseed meal or 3 lbs. hoof and horn meal	**(.5)** 2.5 lbs. bone or 5 lbs. phosphate rock	**(.4)** 1 lb. kelp plus 3.33 lbs. greensand or 5 lbs. granite; or 5.33 lbs. greensand; or 8 lbs. granite
Very Low	**(.5)** 4 lbs. blood meal or 5 lbs. fish meal or 10 lbs. cottonseed meal or 4 lbs. hoof and horn meal	**(.6)** 3 lbs. bone or 6 lbs. phosphate rock	**(.5)** 1 lb. kelp plus 4 lbs. greensand or 6 lbs. granite; or 6.66 lbs. greensand; or 10 lbs. granite

8. Addition of nutriment at these levels is optimal. You need not add any, but the health and yields of your plants may be noticeably increased if you do.

9. Because of the growth hormones kelp meal contains, do not add more than 1 pound per 100 square feet per year.

pH

Most vegetables grow best in a slightly acidic pH of 6.5. A range of 6.0 to 7.5 is fine for most crops. When adequate organic matter is used, we have found crops will tolerate better a wider range of acidity or alkalinity.

To lower the pH one point, use 2 cubic feet aged manure per 100 square feet (about 68 pounds, or a 1/4 inch layer over the area to be planted). Optimally, do not use more than 4 cubic feet of manure per year (about 136 pounds, or a 1/2 inch layer). This is because the salts from the urine it contains can build up in the soil over time. It is best to use manure which contains little sawdust. Sawdust steals nitrogen from the plants during the period in which it breaks down into compost.

To raise the pH one point use the following amount of Dolomitic Lime:

> Light, sandy soil—5 pounds per 100 square feet
> Sandy Loam—7 pounds
> Loam (good soil)—10 pounds
> Silt and Clay Loam (somewhat clayey soil)—12 pounds.

The table on page 20 describes the nutriment content of many commonly used organic fertilizers. You can also use it to determine which fertilizers to add and in what amounts by using the pure nutriment information amounts in the table on page 18. In your calculations, you may also *subtract* nutriment added in the form of manure (if any) during the pH modification. Be careful about subtracting nitrogen, however, as much aged manure in actuality often contains little nitrogen and a substantial amount of nitrogen-borrowing sawdust. If you use a lot of manure containing sawdust, as a pH modifier or soil texturizer, you may want to add about 1 extra pound of blood, fish or hoof and horn meal or 2 extra pounds cotton seed meal per 100 square feet. You may also subtract nutriment added in the form of compost, if you have performed a soil test on the compost and know its nutriment values. Notice that the release times are different for each fertilizer. Sometimes we use a combination of blood meal (which releases over a 3-4 month period), fish meal (which releases over a 6-8 month period), and hoof and horn meal (which releases over a 12 month period). In this way, nitrogen release is spread over a longer period of time. For example, if a soil test indicated we needed 0.4 pounds of pure nitrogen per 100 square feet, we might add:

1 pound blood meal	&	1 pound fish meal	&	1 pound hoof and horn meal
.125 pounds N (12.5%)		.105 pounds N (10.5%)		.140 pounds N (14%)

.125
.105
.140
____
.370 pounds N or approximately the .4 pounds N needed

ANALYSIS OF RECOMMENDED ORGANIC SOIL AMENDMENTS

N, P and K refer to the three main nutrients plants need: NITROGEN for green growth and in compost piles to speed decomposition, PHOSPHORUS for root growth, disease resistance, and production of good fruits, vegetables, and flowers, and POTASH for strong stems, vigorous roots and increased disease resistance. Plants also need HUMUS which is provided by decomposed organic matter such as compost and manure. For information on the application rates for organic fertilizers when a soil test is not used, see the Fertilizer Program Table which follows this table.

NITROGEN

Cottonseed Meal

3-5% N   2% P   1% K   Lasts 4-6 months. Use up to 10 lbs/100 sq. ft. Fair source of nitrogen. Especially good for citrus and azaleas because it has an acidifying effect on soil.

Blood Meal

12.5% N   1.3% P   .7% K   Lasts 3-4 months. Use up to 5 lbs./100 sq. ft. A quick acting source of nitrogen, good for slow compost piles. Can burn plants if using more than 3 lbs. per 100 square feet. If using higher amounts, wait 2 weeks to plant.

Hoof & Horn Meal

14% N   2% P   0% K   Lasts 12 months. Use up to 4 lbs./200 sq. ft. Highest nitrogen source. Slow releasing: no noticeable results for 4-6 weeks.

Fish Meal

10.5% N   6% P   0% K   Lasts 6-8 months. Use up to 5 lbs./100 sq. ft. Good combined nitrogen and phosphorus source.

PHOSPHORUS

Bone Meal

3% N   20% P   0% K   Lasts 6 months to 1 year. Use up to 5 lbs. Excellent source of phosphorus. Especially good on roses, around bulbs, and around fruit trees and flower beds.

Phosphate Rock

33% P   Lasts 3-5 years. Use up to 10 lbs./100 sq. ft. Very slow releasing.

Soft Phosphate

18% P   Lasts 2-3 years. Use up to 10 lbs./100 sq. ft. Clay base makes it more available to plants than the phosphorus in phosphate rock, though the two are used interchangeably.

POTASH

Kelp Meal

1% N   0% P   12% K   33% minerals. Lasts 6 months to 1 year. Excellent source of potash, iron, and other minerals. Kelp meal is also a natural fungicide. Use sparingly (up to 1 pound per 100 square feet per year) because it contains growth hormones.

Wood Ashes

1-10% K   Lasts 6 months. Use up to 1-2 lbs./100 sq. ft. Ashes from wood are high in potash and help repel root maggots. Ashes also have an alkaline effect on the soil, so use them with care. Black wood ash is best.

Crushed Granite

3-5% K   Lasts up to 10 years. Use up to 10 lbs./100 sq. ft. Good slow-releasing source of potash and trace minerals.

Greensand

0% N   1.5% P   6.7% K   Use interchangeably with crushed granite.

SOIL pH SCALE

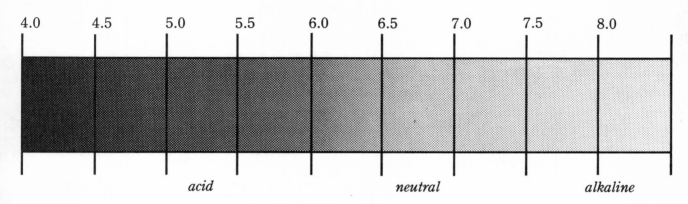

A pH reading tells you the relative acidity/alkalinity of the soil. Most vegetables will grow well in a range from 6.0 to 7.5. 6.5 is probably the best all round pH. In extremely acid or extremely alkaline soils valuable nutrients are tied up and thus unavailable to the plants. An acid soil can be sweetened by the addition of dolomite lime. An alkaline soil can be brought closer to neutral by compost or manure. Compost has a buffering effect on soil, correcting both acid and alkaline conditions.

SOIL MODIFIERS

Dolomitic Lime

A good source of calcium and magnesium to be used in acid soils. Do not use lime to "sweeten" the compost pile; it results in a serious loss of nitrogen. You can discourage flies and odors with a layer of soil.

Gypsum

Gypsum is not needed by organic gardeners. It is normally used commercially in soils made impermeable by excess exchangeable sodium.

"Clodbuster"

15% Humic Acid   5.5 pH   Lasts 1 year. Use up to 1 lb./100 sq. ft.

Eggshells

High in calcium. Especially good for cabbage family crops. Helps break up clay and release nutrients tied up in alkaline soils. Use up to 2 lbs/100 sq. ft.

Manure

An excellent mulch and good source of humus in the garden. Nutriment levels depend on proper handling and the amount of straw or sawdust present. Large amounts of bedding may add up to 2 years to the decomposition time. 50 pounds of manure (approx. 2 cubic feet dry weight) applied per 100 square feet can lower the pH *one* point.

Horse	.7%N	.3%P	.6%K	Age 2-3 months
Rabbit	2.4	1.4	.6	Age 2 months
Chicken	1.1	.8	.5	Age 2 months
Steer	.7	.3	.4	Age 2 years

Compost

Good compost is the most important part of the garden. It aerates soil, breaks up clay, binds together sand, improves drainage, prevents erosion, neutralizes toxins, holds precious moisture, releases essential nutriments, and feeds the microbiotic life of the soil, creating healthy conditions for natural antibiotics, worms and beneficial fungi. Use an inch of compost each year (8 cu. ft./100 sq. ft.) or up to three inches in a first-year garden.

What a Soil Test Will Not Tell You.

A soil test is a limited tool and points out deficiencies of major nutrients. If you simply can't get plants to come up in your garden, a soil test may not give you the solution. Plants lacking only major nutriments will usually grow and show their deficiency in yellowed leaves, stunted growth, purple veins or any of a number of signs.

When seeds fail to germinate, or plants hardly grow at all after germination, some common causes are:

1.   Use of redwood compost. As a mulch or soil conditioner redwood compost is widely available, but it does contain growth inhibitors that can keep seeds from coming up or keep plants from growing well. (This is how the redwood trees reduce competition.)

2.   Planting too early or too late in the season. Seeds will wait for the right temperature and length of day to start growth.

3.   Use of weed killers or soil sterilants. Many weed killers are short-lived but they can limit growth in a garden long after they are supposed to degrade. Soil sterilants can last for two years. Some people use them to minimize or eliminate yard care, but they can continue to have an effect after the users move away and you move in. There is never any reason to use these poisons in your yard. Also, dumping excess motor oil can destroy valuable growing areas. Take it to a service station for recycling.

4. Use of old seeds. Check with your source.

GENERAL FERTILIZER PROGRAM—PER CROP

Assuming no soil test is performed

Functions	Sources	1st & 2nd yr. Assuming poor soil	3rd & 4th yr. Or 1st & 2nd yr. in average soil	5th yr. Or 1st year in good soil	Maintenance Every year thereafter[12]	Add to Soil *before* or *after* Double-Dig
Nitrogen	Cottonseed Meal (or Fish Meal) (or Blood Meal)[10] (or Hoof & Horn Meal)	10 lbs. (5 lbs.) (5 lbs.) (4 lbs.)	6 lbs. (3 lbs.) (3 lbs.) (2 lbs.)	3 lbs. (1-2 lbs.) (1-2 lbs.) (1 lb.)	— — — —	After
Phosphorous	Bone Meal (or Phosphate Rock or Soft Phosphate)	4-5 lbs. (10 lbs.)	2 lbs. (5 lbs.)	2 lbs. (3 lbs.)	2 lbs. —	After
Potash and Trace Minerals	Kelp Meal and Wood Ash (or Granite or Greensand)	1 lb. 2 lbs. (10 lbs.)	1 lb. 1 lb. (5 lbs.)	1 lb. 1 lb. (3 lbs.)	1/4 lb.[13] 1 lb. —	After
Texturizer, Microbiotic Life, Humus, Multiple Nutriments	Manure	2 cu. ft.	2 cu. ft.	2 cu. ft.	2 cu. ft.	After
	Compost	Up to 1 cu. yd. (1st crop), 8 cu. ft. (ea. addit. crop)[11]	8 cu. ft.	8 cu. ft.	8 cu. ft.	Before
Calcium	Eggshells	2 lbs.	1 lb.	as available up to 1/2 lb.		After
Humic Acid	"Clodbuster"	1 lb.	—	—	—	After

10. Do not plant for 2 weeks if using more than 3 pounds blood meal per 100 sq. ft. It can burn the plants during this time since it releases nitrogen rapidly at first.

11. 1 cubic yard equals 27 cubic feet. 1 cubic yard will cover 100 sq. ft. 3″ deep. 8 cubic feet will cover 100 sq. ft. 1″ deep. 2 cubic feet will cover 10(sq. ft. 1/4″ deep. You can substitute manure for compost the first year if you do not have a ready supply of compost.

12. Beginning the sixth year your legumes, cover crops, and recycled plant materials (in the form of compost) can provide most of your nitrogen, phosphorous and potash. Double-check this periodically with a soil test.

13. For trace minerals: kelp meal is 33% trace minerals.

To revitalize an old lawn—Use 1.5 lbs. hoof and horn meal, 2 lbs. bone meal, and 1 lb. kelp meal per 100 sq. ft. Apply in spring and water well twice a week for 2 weeks. You should see the results in 6 weeks.

Fruit trees—Use 1 heaping tablespoon blood meal per foot of height, up to 2 lbs. of bone meal per full grown tree, and a light sprinkling of kelp meal (up to 1/4 lb. per full grown tree) around the drip line. Apply in spring when leaves first start to appear and water in well. Cover crops and compost mulches are also excellent for full grown trees.

Citrus trees—Same as fruit trees with the addition of 5-8 lbs. phosphate rock and 2 lbs. of Clodbuster applied to full grown trees once every 3-5 years. Line the planting hole with crushed red rock for a long-lasting source of iron.

The bed should be shaped before the fertilizers are added. If your soil is in good condition, use a rake to shape the bed into a mound as shown below. The soil will not easily wash off or erode from beds shaped in this manner, once the texture and structure of the soil are improved. While you are still improving the texture of heavy, clay soils, you may want to form a *flat-topped bed* with a small lip on the other edges of the bed instead. This will minimize watering-caused erosion. It is also desirable to provide the sides of the beds with a 45 degree slope. A sharper angle will encourage erosion. When the bed has been shaped, tamp the soil down before planting by placing the digging board on all parts of the bed and walking across the board. If a lip is added to the bed, it is done after the soil is tamped down.

(Left) raking soil out from inside lip.
(Right) raking soil up from side for lip.

Add the fertilizers and other additives one at a time after the bed has been dug and shaped. Avoid windy days and hold fertilizer close to the bed surface when spreading. Use the different colors to help you. The soil is darkish so sprinkle a light colored fertilizer (such as bone meal) on first, then a dark one (such as kelp meal) and so on. It is better to under apply the fertilizers because you can go back over the bed afterwards to spread any left over but it is difficult to pick up fertilizer if too much falls in one place. Aim for even distribution. After all are applied, sift in the fertilizers and other additives by inserting a spading fork 2-3 inches deep and lifting it upwards with a slight jiggling motion.

Several things should be noted about the special nature of the nutriments added in the upper 2 to 3 inches of the soil. 1) The nutriments are added to the upper layer as in nature. 2) The nutriments percolate downward with the root growth of the plant. 3) Organic fertilizers break down more slowly than most chemical fertilizers and therefore remain available to the plants for a longer period of time.

The bone meal often used in the upper layer provides quality growth-producing phosphorus and calcium to the plants plus an important animal essence. Wood ash (preferably black wood ash) provides strength, plant essence, aids in insect control and is a flavor enhancer for vegetables, especially lettuce and tomatoes. Black wood ash is produced from a controlled, soil covered, slow-burning fire built during a soft drizzle or rain. This ash is higher in potash and other minerals because they do not readily escape into the atmosphere as the wood is consumed

(Left) casting fertilizer onto bed surface. (Right) sifting in fertilizers with spading fork.

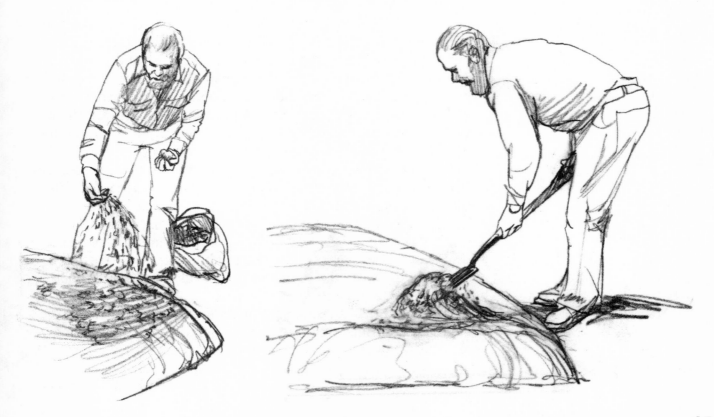

by fire. Wood ashes should be stored in a tight container until they are used. Exposure to light and air will destroy much of their nutriment value. Ashes from a fireplace may be used if they are from wood and not paper.

Manure is a microbiotic life stimulant and an animal and plant essence that has been "composted" both inside the animal and outside in a curing pile. Avoid using too much manure because steer and horse manures (which do not contain much sawdust or straw) are generally 2 parts nitrogen to 1 part phosphorous and 1 part potash, and contain an excess of salts. This is an unbalanced ratio in favor of nitrogen which in time results in weak and rank plant growth more susceptible to disease and insect attack. A ratio of 1 part nitrogen to 1 part phosphorous to 1 part potash is better. The biodynamic/French intensive method always uses as much or more phosphorous and potash as nitrogen in the fertilization process. This approach results in stronger and healthier plants. The use of a large amount of manure is recommended as an alternative to compost only when compost is not available. This is one way in which the combined biodynamic/French intensive techniques differ from the initial French intensive dependence on horse manure.

The heavy emphasis which the biodynamic/French intensive method places on compost should be noted. The demand for most organic fertilizers is going up while the supply available to each person in the world is decreasing. Soon, few fertilizers will be available at reasonable prices. Also, the materials used for the production of chemical fertilizers are becoming less available. Materials for biodynamic/French intensive method compost, on the other hand, consist of plants, animals and earth which can be produced in a sustained way by *living* soils. These compostable materials can be produced indefinitely if we take care of our soils and do not exhaust them. In fact, 96% of the total amount of nutriments needed for good plant growth processes can be obtained as plant and microbiotic life forms work on elements already in the air.[14] Soil and compost can provide the rest.

The biodynamic/French intensive method has its roots 3000 years into the past in Chinese intensive agriculture, 2000 years into the past in the Greek use of raised beds and more recently in European farming. Similar practices are still used today in the native agriculture of many countries, such as Guatemala. "The method" will extend its roots into a future where environmentally balanced resource usage is of the utmost importance. Compost made according to "the method" (the process will be discussed in the section on Compost) is usually high in phosphorous, potash and trace minerals. It also contains a small amount of nitrogen and, when made with nitrogen-fixing cover crops, can be high in nitrogen. Nitrogen is also obtained from the thin layer of manure added during the fertilization stage. Lastly, nitrogen

14. Joseph A. Cocannouer, *Farming With Nature,* University of Oklahoma Press, Norman, Oklahoma, 1954, p. 50.

is obtained for the garden system by the periodic growing of legumes such as peas, beans, clover, alfalfa and vetch in the planting beds. The nitrogen that they fix from the air is released in the decomposition of their roots, stems and leaves. Compost, bone meal, manure, wood ash, nitrogen from legumes and nutriments from the growth of certain kinds of weeds in the beds (which is discussed in the section on Companion Planting) make up the 4% of the plant diet not provided by the air.

The Balanced Eco-system. Nothing happens in living nature that is not in relation to the whole.

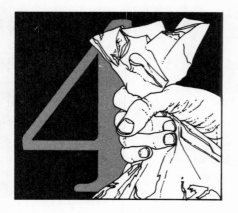

Compost

In nature, living things die and their death allows life to be reborn. Both animals and plants die on forest floors and in meadows to be composted by time, water, microorganisms, sun and air to produce a soil improved in texture and nutriment. Organic agriculture follows nature's example. Leaves, grass, spiders, birds, trees and plants should be returned to the soil and reused—not thrown away. Composting is an important way to recycle such elements as carbon, nitrogen, oxygen, sulfur, calcium, iron, phosphorous, potash, trace minerals and microorganisms. These elements are all necessary to maintain the biological cycles of life that exist in nature. All too often we participate instead in agricultural stripmining

Composting in nature occurs in at least three ways: 1) In the form of manures, which are plant and animal foods composted inside the body of an animal (including earthworms) and then further aged outside the animal by the heat of fermentation. Earthworms are especially good composters. Their castings are 5 times richer in nitrogen, 2 times richer in exchangeable calcium, 7 times richer in available phosphorous and 11 times richer in available potassium than the soil they inhabit. 2) In the form of animal and plant bodies which decay on top of the soil in nature and in compost piles. 3) In the form of roots, root hairs and microbiotic life which remain and decay beneath the surface of the soil after harvesting. It is estimated that one rye plant in good soil grows 3 miles of roots a day, 387 miles of roots in a season and 6,603 miles of root hairs each season![15]

Compost has a dual function. It improves the structure of the soil. This means the soil will be easier to work, will have

15. Helen Philbrick and Richard B. Gregg, *Companion Plants and How To Use Them,* The Devin-Adair Company, Old Greenwich, Connecticut, 1966, pp. 75-76.

A CROSS SECTION OF THE FOREST FLOOR

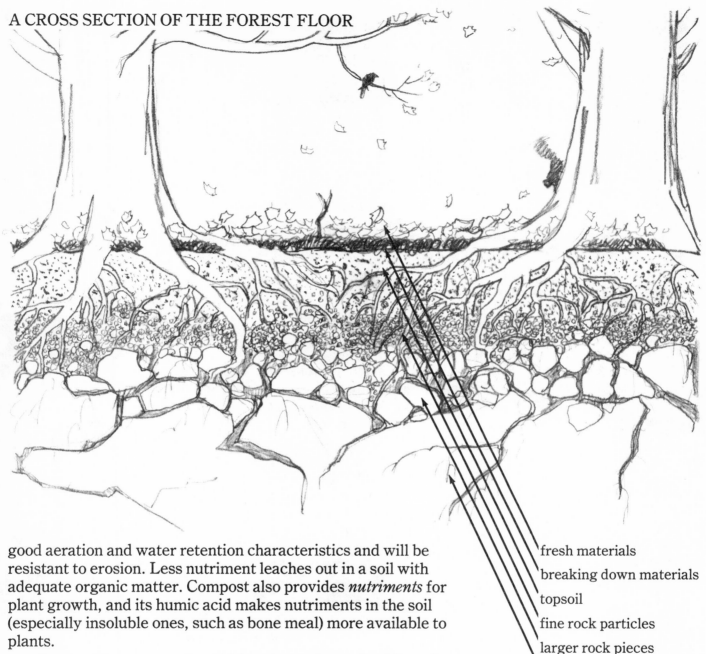

fresh materials
breaking down materials
topsoil
fine rock particles
larger rock pieces
rock

good aeration and water retention characteristics and will be resistant to erosion. Less nutriment leaches out in a soil with adequate organic matter. Compost also provides *nutriments* for plant growth, and its humic acid makes nutriments in the soil (especially insoluble ones, such as bone meal) more available to plants.

Improved texture and nourishment produce a healthy soil. A healthy soil produces healthy plants better able to resist insect and disease attacks due in part to a higher protein content in the plants. Most insects look for sick plants to eat—those plants with a relatively higher carbohydrate content. The best way to control insects and diseases in plants is with a living, healthy soil rather than with poisons which kill this life.

Compost keeps soil at maximum health with a minimum of expense. Generally, it is unnecessary to buy fertilizers in order to be able to grow with nature. At first, organic fertilizers may have to be purchased so that the soil can be brought to a satisfactory level of fertility in a short period of time. Once this has been done, the health of the soil can be maintained with compost, crop rotation, and small amounts of manure, bone meal and wood ash.

Compost is high in humus and humic acid. Humus results from the decomposing and synthesizing activities of organisms in organic matter. The importance of adding soil at various stages to your compost pile is clear. The soil contains a good starter supply of these organisms. The organisms help in several ways. Some break down complex compounds into simpler ones the plants can utilize. One soil bacterium, azotobacter, converts atmospheric nitrogen into food for plants. Other microorganisms tie up nitrogen surpluses. The surpluses are released gradually as the plants need nitrogen. An excessive concentration of available nitrogen in the soil (which makes plants susceptible to disease) is therefore avoided. There are predaceous fungi which attack and devour nematodes, but they are only found in large amounts in a soil with adequate humus.

The microbiotic life provide a living pulsation in the soil which preserves its vitality for the plants. The microbes tie up essential nutriments in their own body tissues as they grow, and then release them slowly as they die and decompose. In this way, they help stabilize food release to the plants. These organisms are also continuously excreting a whole range of organic compounds into the soil. Sometimes described as "soil glue", these excretions help hold the soil structure together. The organic compounds also contain disease-curing antibiotics, health producing vitamins and enzymes that are integral parts of biochemical reactions in a healthy soil.

It is important to note the difference between *fertilization* and *fertility*. There can be plenty of fertilizer in the soil and plants still may not grow well. Add compost to the soil and the humic acid it contains begins to release the hidden nutriment in a form available to the plants. This was the source of the amazing fertility of Alan Chadwick's garden at Santa Cruz.

The recipe for a biodynamic/French Intensive Method compost is *by weight:* 1/3 *dry vegetation,* 1/3 *green vegetation and kitchen wastes,* and 1/3 *soil*—though we have found with our heavy clay soil that less soil produces better results. The ground underneath the pile should be loosened to a depth of 12-24 inches to expose the bottom layer of the pile to the bacteria and organisms in the soil and to provide good drainage. The materials should be added to the pile in 1-2 inch layers with the dry vegetation on the bottom, the green vegetation and kitchen wastes second and the soil third (a 1/4-1/2 inch layer). Green vegetation is 95 percent more effective than dry vegetation as a "starter" because its higher nitrogen content helps start and maintain the fermentation process. Dry vegetation is high in carbon content. It is difficult for the compost pile to digest carbon without sufficient amounts of nitrogen. Unless you have a large household it may be necessary to save your kitchen scraps in a tight-lidded unbreakable container for several days to get enough material for the kitchen waste layer. Hold your breath when you dump them because the stronger smelling form of anaerobic decom-

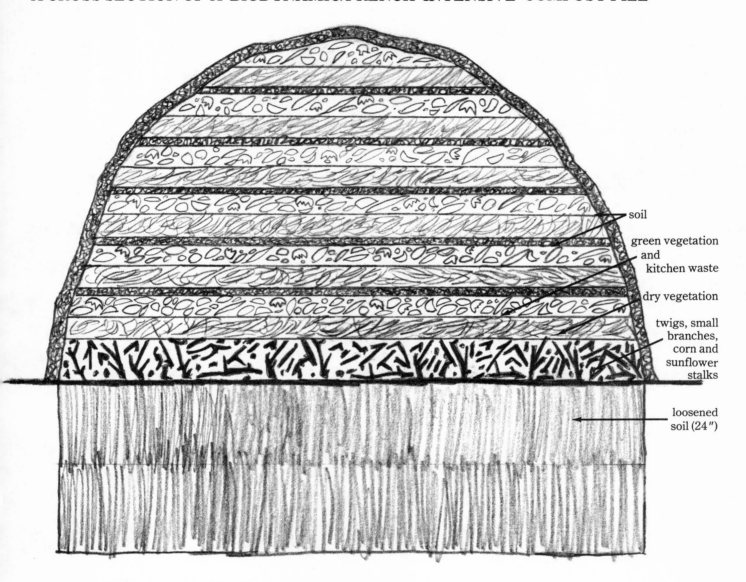

soil

green vegetation
and
kitchen waste

dry vegetation

twigs, small
branches,
corn and
sunflower
stalks

loosened
soil (24″)

position process will be accelerated by the already fermenting waste. All kitchen scraps may be added to this layer except meats and sizeable amounts of oily salad scraps. Be sure to include bones, tea leaves, coffee grounds and citrus rinds.

Add the soil immediately after the kitchen waste. It contains microorganisms which speed decomposition, keeps the smell down to a minor level and prevents flies from laying eggs in the garbage. The smell will be difficult to eliminate entirely when waste from members of the cabbage family is added. In a few days, however, even this soil minimized odor will disappear. As each layer is added, water it lightly so the pile is *evenly* moist— like a wrung-out damp towel that is entirely wet, but does not give out excess water when it is squeezed. Sufficient water is necessary for the proper heating and decomposition of the materials. Too little water results in decreased biological activity and too much simply drowns the aerobic microbiotic life. Water the pile when necessary as you water the garden. The particles in

Soil is added to compost pile after green vegetation and kitchen waste layer.

The least expensive type of compost container

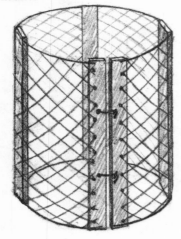

Four kinds of compost piles

pallet type

pile

modular box type

large wire-fabric type

the pile should glisten. During the rainy season some shelter or covering may be needed to prevent overwatering and the less optimal anaerobic decomposition that occurs in a water-logged pile. (The conditions needed for proper functioning of a compost pile and those required for good plant growth in raised beds are similar. In both cases the proper mixture of air, soil nutriments, texture, microorganisms and water is essential.)

Compost piles can be built in a pit in the ground or in a pile above the ground. The latter is preferable, since during rainy periods a pit can fill up with water. A pile can be made with or without a container. A container is not necessary, but can help shape a pile and keep the materials looking neat. The least expensive container is made of 12 foot long, 3 foot wide, 1 inch mesh, chicken wire with five 3 foot long, 1 inch by 2 inch boards and two sets of small hooks and eyes. The boards are nailed along the two 3 foot ends of the wire and at 3 foot intervals along the length of the wire (see illustration). The hooks and eyes are attached to the two end boards near the top and bottom. The unit is then placed as a circle on the ground, the hooks attached to the eyes, and the compost materials placed inside. The materials hold up the circle. After the pile is built, the wire enclosure may be removed and the materials will stay in place. You may now use the enclosure to build another pile, or you may use it later to turn the first pile into, if you decide to turn it to speed the decomposition process.

There are three ways to speed up the decomposition rate in a compost pile. One way is to *increase the amount of nitrogen.* The ratio of carbon to nitrogen is critical for the breakdown rate. Materials with a high carbon to nitrogen ratio, such as wood, may take years to decompose alone since they lack sufficient nitrogen-bearing materials upon which the bacteria depend for food. Such materials are sawdust, dry leaves, wood shavings, grainstubble and straw. To boost the rate of decay in carbonaceous materials, add nitrogen-rich materials such as newly cut grass, fresh manure, vegetable wastes, green vegetation or a fertilizer such as blood or fish meal. Three to five pounds of blood or fish meal per cubic yard of compost is probably a good amount of fertilizer with which to fortify a compost pile with a high carbon content. These fertilizers are lightly sprinkled on each layer as the pile is built.

A second method is to *increase the amount of air* (aeration). Beneficial aerobic bacteria thrive in a well aerated pile. Proper layering and periodic turning of the pile will accomplish this. Third, the *surface area of the materials may be increased.* The smaller the size of the materials, the greater the amount of their exposed surface area. Broken up twigs will decompose more rapidly than when twigs are left whole. We discourage the use of shredders because nature will do the job in a relatively short time and everyone has sufficient access to materials which will compost rapidly without resorting to a shredder. The noise from these machines is quite disturbing and spoils the peace and quiet of a garden. They also consume increasingly scarce fuel.

Note that at least *three different materials of three different textures* are used in the biodynamic/French intensive method compost recipe and other recipes. The varied texture will allow good drainage and aeration in the pile. The compost will also have a more diverse nutriment content. A pile made primarily of leaves or grass cuttings makes the passage of water and air through the pile difficult because both tend to mat. Both good air and water penetration are required for proper decomposition. The layering of the materials further promotes a mixture of textures and nutriments and helps insure even decomposition.

A minimum pile size of 3 feet by 3 feet by 3 feet (1 cubic yard weighing about 1000 pounds) is recommended. Smaller piles fail to provide the insulation necessary for proper heating (up to 160 degrees) and allow the penetration of too much air. It is all right to build piles up slowly to this size as materials become available, though it is best to build an entire pile at one time. A pile will cure to 1/2 to 1/3 its original size, depending on the materials used. A large pile size might be 6 feet high, 6 feet wide and 12 feet long.

The best time to prepare compost is in the *spring or autumn* when biological activity is highest. (Too much heat or cold slows down and even kills the microbiotic life in the pile.) The two high activity periods conveniently coincide with the maximum availability of materials in the spring, as grass and other plants begin to grow rapidly, and in the autumn, as leaves fall and other plant life begins to die. The pile should optimally be built under a deciduous oak tree. This tree's nature provides the conditions for the development of excellent soil underneath it. And compost is a kind of soil. The second best place is under another deciduous tree. As a last resort, evergreen trees may be used. The shade and windbreak provided by the trees also help keep the pile at an even moisture level. (The pile should be placed 6 feet away from the tree's trunk so it will not provide a haven for potentially harmful insects.)

Compost is ready to use when it is dark and rich looking. You should not be able to discern the original source of the materials from the texture and the materials should crumble in your hands. Mature compost even smells good—like water in a forest spring! A biodynamic/French intensive pile should be ready to use in 2-1/2 to 3 months. Usually, no turning is needed as the materials used and their layering allow for good aeration and complete breakdown. Compost for use in flats should be passed through a sieve of 1/2 inch or 1/4 inch wire fabric. In the garden a *minimum* maintenance dressing of 1/2 pound of compost per square foot should be added to the soil before each crop. Guidelines for *general* maintenance dressings are a 1 inch layer of compost or 8 cubic feet of compost per 100 square feet (about 3 pounds per square foot).

The biodynamic/French intensive method of compost making differs in particular from the biodynamic method[16] in that it is simpler to prepare, normally uses no manure and usually uses no herbal solutions to stimulate microorganism growth. Weeds, such as stinging nettle, and plants, such as fava beans, are sometimes added in the preparation of special piles, however. Special mixtures are created to meet particular pH, texture and nutriment requirements. Separate compost piles are made of small tree branches since they can take two years to decompose.

The biodynamic/French intensive method of making compost differs from the Rodale compost method[17] in the use of little or no manure and usually no rock powder fertilizers or nitrogen supplements. As mentioned before, manure used continually and in large amounts, is an imbalanced fertilizer, although it is a good texturizing agent because of its usual decomposed sawdust content. When fertilizers are added to a compost pile much of their nutriment value can leach out by the time the pile

16. For the biodynamic method of compost preparation, see pages 37 to 51 in *The Pfeiffer Garden Book,* Alice Heckel (Ed.), Biodynamic Farming and Gardening Association, Inc., Stroudsburg, Pennsylvania, 1967.

17. For the Rodale method of compost preparation, see pages 59 to 86 in *The Basic Book of Organic Gardening,* Robert Rodale (Ed.), Ballentine Books, New York, 1971.

is ready to use. The nitrogen supplements do, however, speed up the decomposition process. Both the biodynamic and Rodale methods are good ones, proven by use over a long period of time. Chadwick's recipe seems simpler to use and equally effective.

Some people use *sheet composting* (a process of spreading uncomposted organic materials over the soil and then digging them into the soil where they decompose). The disadvantage of this method is that the soil should not be planted for 3 months or so until decomposition has occurred. Soil bacteria tie up the nitrogen during the decomposition process, thereby making it unavailable to the plants. Sheet composting is beneficial if it is used during the winter in cold areas, because the tie-up prevents the nitrogen from leaching out during winter rains.

Other people use *green manure composting* (the growing of cover crops such as vetch, clover, alfalfa, bean, pea or other legumes until just before maturity when the plants are dug into the soil). This is an excellent way to bring unworked soil into a reasonable condition. Cover crops are rich in nitrogen, so they boost the nutriment quality of the soil without one's having to resort to the purchase of fertilizers. Their stems and leaves contain a lot of nitrogen and their roots support nitrogen-fixing bacteria. These bacteria take nitrogen from the air and fix it in nodules on the roots, which you can see when you pull the plants up. They also help you dig. Their roots loosen the soil and eventually turn into humus beneath the earth. Fava beans are exceptionally good for green manuring if you plan to plant tomatoes, because their decomposed bodies help eradicate tomato wilt organisms from the soil.

Due to their high nitrogen content, cover crops decompose rapidly. Planting can usually follow one month after the plants are dug into the soil. The disadvantage of the green manuring process is that the land is out of production during the period of cover crop growth and the shorter one month period of decomposition. In some areas, the long term improvement in the soil's nutritive content and structure compensates for this limitation. The advantage of the small-scale biodynamic/French intensive method is that composting still is feasible. Even if you decide to use their produce and not to dig cover crops in, the growing process will put nitrogen into the soil and will make it possible to grow plants such as corn and tomatoes, which are heavy feeders. (see Companion Planting section.) And the plant residues may be used in the compost pile.

Some materials should not be used in the preparation of compost:

☐ Plants infected with a disease or a severe insect attack where eggs could be preserved or where the insects themselves could survive in spite of the compost pile's heat.

☐ Poisonous plants, such as oleander, hemlock, and castor bean, which harm soil life.

- [ ] Plants which take too long to break down, such as magnolia leaves.

- [ ] Plants which have acids toxic to other plants, such as eucalyptus leaves.

- [ ] Plants which may be too acidic or contain substances that interfere with the decomposition process, such as pine needles. Pine needles are extremely acidic and contain a form of kerosene. (Special compost piles are often made of acidic materials, such as pine needles and leaves, however. This compost will lower the soil's pH and stimulate acid loving plants like strawberries.)

- [ ] Ivy and succulents, which may not be killed in the heat of the decomposition process and can regrow when the compost is placed in a planting bed.

- [ ] Pernicious weeds such as wild morning glory and bermuda grass, which will probably not be killed in the decomposition process and which will choke out other plants when they re-sprout after the compost is placed in a planting bed.

- [ ] Cat and dog manures, which can contain pathogens harmful to children. These pathogens are not always killed in the heat of the compost pile.

Plants infected with disease or insects and pernicious weeds should be burned to be properly destroyed. Their ash then becomes a good fertilizer. The ash will also help control harmful soil insects, such as carrot worms, which shy away from the alkalinity of ashes.

Parts of a regular compost pile, which have not broken down completely by the end of the composting period, should be placed on the bottom of a new pile. This is especially true for twigs and small branches which can use the extra protection of the pile's height to speed their decomposition in a situation of increased warmth and moisture.

FUNCTIONS OF COMPOST

Improved Structure—breaks up clay and clods, and binds together sandy soil. Helps make proper aeration in clayey and sandy soil possible.

Moisture Retention—holds 6 times its own weight in water. A soil with good organic matter content soaks up rain like a sponge and regulates the supply to plants. A soil stripped of organic matter resists water penetration thus leading to destructive compaction, erosion and flooding.

Aeration—plants can obtain 96% of the nutrients they need from the *air!* A loose healthy soil assists the exchange of nutrients and moisture. Carbon dioxide released by humus decomposition diffuses out of the soil and is absorbed by the canopy of leaves above in a raised bed mini-climate.

Fertilization—compost contains some nitrogen, phosphorus and potassium but is especially important for trace elements. The important principle is to return to the earth all which has been taken out by the use of plant residues and manures.

pH Buffer—a good compost will lower the pH of an alkaline soil and raise the pH of an acid soil.

Soil Toxin Neutralizer—important recent studies show that plants grown in organically composted soils take up less lead and other urban pollutants.

Nutriment Release—humic acids dissolve soil minerals and make them available to plants. As humus decomposes, it releases nutriments for plant uptake and for the soil microlife population.

Food for Microbiotic Life—good compost creates healthy conditions for soil organisms that live in the soil. Compost harbors earthworms and beneficial fungi that fight nematodes and other soil pests.

The Ultimate in Recycling—the earth provides us food, clothing, shelter, and we close the cycle in offering fertility, health, life through the shepherding of materials.

BUILDING A COMPOST PILE STEP-BY-STEP

1. Loosen soil under the pile area 12 inches deep with a spading fork.

2. Lay down *roughage* (brush, corn stalks or other material) 6 inches thick for air circulation, if they are available.

3. Put down 2 inch layer of *garden waste*—weeds, leaves, grass clippings.

4. Save up *kitchen waste* and dump over layer of garden waste. Cover lightly with *soil* to prevent flies and odors.

5. Add a new layer of garden waste, kitchen waste and soil as materials become available until pile is 3 to 6 feet high.

6. Let completed pile cure 3 to 6 months while building a new pile.

7. Water completed pile regularly until ready for use. For planning purposes, remember that a 6 foot high compost pile will be only 2 to 3 feet high when it is ready to use.

Note: Materials with a high carbon content such as leaves, dry weeds and grass clippings, sawdust and wood chips are very slow to decompose, taking six months to three years. To hasten decomposition, keep moist and add materials high in nitrogen such as fresh manure or blood meal. Green weeds, fresh grass clippings and juicy kitchen waste are quick to decompose. Alone, these highly nitrogenous materials can break down in as little as two weeks BUT they can attract flies and cause offensive odors unless mixed with high-carbon materials.

Seed Propagation

Now that we know a little about the body and soul of our Earth, we are ready to witness the birth of seedlings. For a minute close your eyes, pretend you are the seed of your favorite plant, tree, vegetable, fruit, flower or herb. You are all alone. You can do nothing in this state. Slowly you begin to hear sounds around you. The wind, perhaps. You feel warmth from the sun—the ground underneath you. What things do you need in relation to you for good growth? Think like a seed and ask yourself what a seed needs in nature—air, warmth, moisture, soil, nutriment, microorganisms. You need these things, at least, along with other plants, birds, insects, spiders, frogs and chickens. You need an entire microcosm of the world.

Generally, the first elements fall into two categories: the terrestrial (soil and nutriment) and the celestial (air, warmth, moisture). These elements cannot be completely categorized, however, since air, warmth and moisture come from the heavens to circulate through the soil and gases can be taken into plants through their roots as well as their leaves. Nutriment on the other hand, can be borne upon the air currents. In fact, the important trace mineral zinc is taken in more readily by citrus tree leaves, than by their roots. The parts that other elements in the plant and animal worlds play—the parts of other plants and insects, for example—will be discussed in the section on Companion Planting.

Seed Planting

Seeds should be planted as deep as the vertical dimension of each seed. Preferably, the seed should be covered with sifted compost, which is similar to decomposed plant matter found

The depth to which a seed is planted is equal to its vertical dimension.

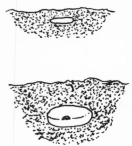

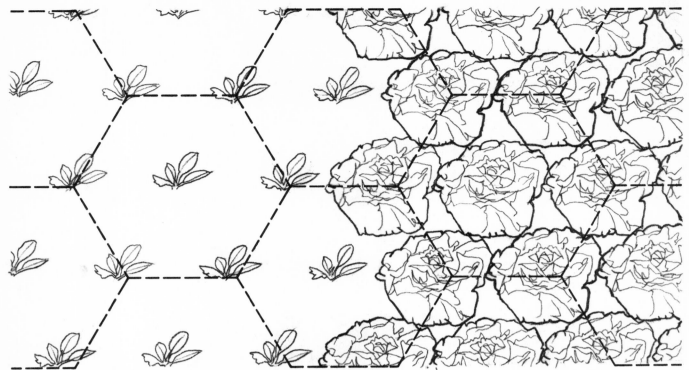

HEXAGONAL SPACING
Head lettuce —12 inch centers

over germinating seeds in nature. This compost stimulates the germination process. Lima and fava beans may be planted on their sides. The root system, which emerges from the eye, will still be able to grow straight down.

The seeds, whether they are planted in beds or flats, should be planted in a diagonally offset or hexagonal spacing pattern with each seed the same distance from all the seeds nearest it. The spacings given in the chart later in this section show how far to place different plants from each other, so that when the plants are mature in the flats or the planting beds their leaves will barely touch and provide the living mulch mini-climate under the leaves so essential to balanced, uninterrupted growth. In general, the plant spacings for vegetables, flowers and herbs are the "within the row" spacings listed on the back of seed packets or sometimes 3/4 of this distance. *Disregard* the "between rows" spacings. Spacing for plants normally grown on hills has to be determined by experimentation. Our best spacings to date for these are given in the spacing charts. Plants spaced accordingly form living mulch, which retards weed growth and aids in the retention of soil moisture by shading the soil. When spacing seeds in flats, place the seeds so far apart that the seedlings' leaves will barely touch when the seedlings are transplanting size. Try 1-inch to 2-inch spacings depending on the size of the seedling at its transplanting stage (see spacing chart at the end of this section).

To make the placement of seeds in the planting beds or flats easier, use frames with 1-inch and 2-inch mesh chicken wire stretched across it. The mesh is built on a hexagonal pattern, so the seeds can be dropped in the center of a hexagon and be on the proper center. Or, if a center greater than 1 inch

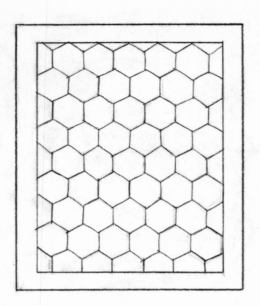

Spacing frame for placing seeds in flats. Place seed in center of each space.

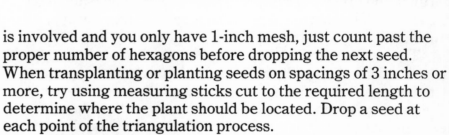

Spacing stick for placing seeds in beds. 3 inch to 36 inch sizes used according to crop planted.

Triangular spacing template for placing seeds in beds.

is involved and you only have 1-inch mesh, just count past the proper number of hexagons before dropping the next seed. When transplanting or planting seeds on spacings of 3 inches or more, try using measuring sticks cut to the required length to determine where the plant should be located. Drop a seed at each point of the triangulation process.

Once you have gotten the feel for plant spacing, you may want to practice broadcasting seeds by hand and eventually graduate to this method of sowing. Broadcasting is the method used by Alan Chadwick and his apprentices in both flats and growing beds. When you reach this stage, seeds should end up 1/4 to 1/2 inch apart in the first flat. This way the seeds can take advantage of complete mini-climate growth stimulation and health earlier in their life. It does require more time to do several transplantings though. When these plants' leaves are barely touching, they should be transplanted into other flats on 1/2 to 1-inch centers. Approximately four flats will be filled by one flat of broadcasted seeds. Or you can broadcast the seeds on 1/2 to 1-inch spacings initially and thin the areas where plants are too close together. Sometimes little thinning is needed. Broadcasting and thinning can also eventually be done in the growing beds. Thinning will probably take the same amount of time (or more) as placing seeds on their proper centers in the first place, but the health of plants from broadcast seeds will probably be better because of an earlier established mini-climate. You will also eventually learn to transplant with fair accuracy without measuring!

Cover the seeds in flats with a layer of the flat soil mixture described below. Seeds in a planting bed should normally be covered with soil taken from the bed itself *after* the double-digging has been completed and *before* the shaping and fertilization steps are begun. Or, large seeds may be poked into the soil to the proper depth with your index finger. The hole may then be filled by pushing soil into it with your thumb and index finger.

Seeding triangulation

Seedling flat construction
Sides and bottom are of bender board

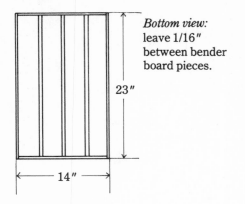

Bottom view:
leave 1/16″
between bender
board pieces.

23″

14″

Ends are of 1″ x 3″, 1″ x 6″, and
1″ x 10″ redwood

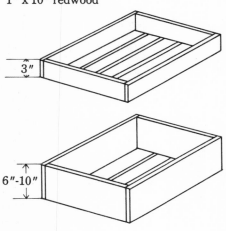

3″

6″-10″

The leaves are roots in the air . . .

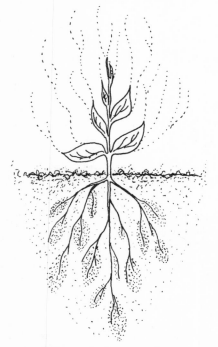

roots are leaves in the ground . . .

Flats

If you build your own flats, the standard flat size is 3 inches deep by 14 inches wide by 23 inches long. The depth is critical since too shallow a depth allows the seedling roots to touch the bottom too soon. When this occurs, the plants believe they have reached the limit of their growth and they enter a state of ''premature senility''. In this state the plants begin to flower and fruit even though they are only transplanting size. We have experienced this with broccoli and dwarf marigolds. The broccoli heads were the size of a little fingernail. The length and width of the flat are not as critical. Their size should not become too large, however, if the flat is to be easy to carry in weight and size. If plants must remain in the container more than 4 to 6 weeks, a container 6 to 10 inches or more in depth should be used.

When planting seeds or seedlings, remember that the most important area for the plant is the 2 inches above and the 2 inches below the surface of the flat or the planting bed. This is because of the mini-climate created under the plants' leaves and because of the important protection of the upper roots in the flat or the bed by the soil. Without proper protection, the plants will develop tough necks at the point where the stem emerges from the soil. A toughened neck slows the flow of plant juices and interrupts and weakens plant growth. These areas are also important because in a very real sense the roots are *leaves in the soil* and the leaves are *roots in the air.* The explanation for this dualism lies in the fact that the roots ''breathe'' in (absorb) gases in significant amounts during certain periods of the month as if they were leaves and that the leaves absorb moisture and nutriment from the air. Also, plant life activity varies above and below the ground according to monthly cycles. Root growth is stimulated more during the third quarter of each 28 day period and leaf growth is stimulated more during the second quarter in accordance with the phases of the moon. (See pages 46-47.)

The exact critical distance above and below the surface of the planting bed is not necessarily 2 inches. Obviously it will be different for radishes than for corn, since their leaves begin at different heights from the soil surface and because they have different depths to their root systems. Generally speaking though, the 2-inch—2-inch guideline helps us develop a sensitivity to the plants' needs above and below ground. (The need for proper conditions above and below ground was also noted in the comparison between the normal use of rows in gardening and farming and the use of raised beds for growing plants on pages 3 and 4). In particular, the mini-climate protects the feeder roots and the microbiotic life which are both concentrated in the upper soil.

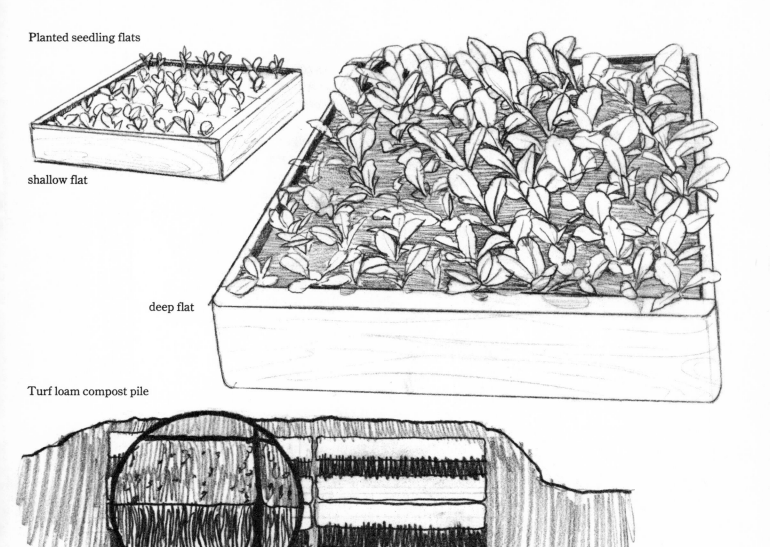

Planted seedling flats

shallow flat

deep flat

Turf loam compost pile

Flat Soil

You are now ready to prepare the soil in which to grow these versatile plants. A good planting mixture to use for starting seeds in flats is 1/3 each compost, sharp (gritty) sand and turf loam. The three ingredients provide a fertile, loose-textured mixture. These elements should be mixed thoroughly together and placed in the flat on top of a 1/8 inch layer of oak leaf mold (partially decayed oak leaves) or compost, which lines the bottom of the flat for drainage and additional nutriment. Crushed egg shells may also be placed above the oak leaf mold for calcium-loving plants such as carnations and members of the cabbage family. The thin egg shell layer should cover one-quarter of the surface. Turf loam is made by composting sections of turf grass grown in good soil. The sections are composted with the grass side of the sections together and the soil sections together within the pile. Good garden soil can be substituted for the turf loam.

Loose soil with good nutriments enables roots to penetrate the soil easily and a steady stream of nutriments flows into the stem and leaves

Hold seedling by leaves.

The hand fork

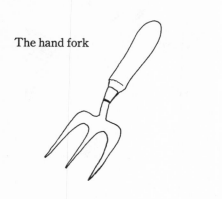

The correct way to unpot a seedling.

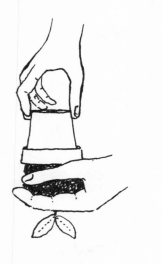

Spread rootbound plant roots out before transplanting into bed.

Transplanting

The biodynamic/French intensive method continually seeks to foster uninterrupted plant growth. Part of this technique is embodied in the "Breakfast-Lunch-Dinner!" concept stressed by Alan Chadwick. Frequently, seedlings are raised in a very good soil—in terms of nutriment and texture—only to be transplanted into an area which has little nutriment and a poor texture. The plant suffers root shock when it is uprooted from the flat and then encounters nutriment deficiency and physical impediment to growth in poor soil. Better results occur when seedlings are transplanted from a flat with a good planting mixture "Breakfast" into a second flat with a "Lunch" consisting of a similar mixture fortified with extra compost. The plant will forget its trauma in tasting the delectable new lunch treats in the second flat. This process minimizes shock and even fosters growth. In the biodynamic/French intensive method, transplanting stimulates growth rather than slowing it down. Finally, a splendid biodynamic/French intensive "Dinner" greets the plant in the growing bed! With this kind care and stimulated healthy plant growth there is less likelihood of insect and disease damage.

A biodynamic gardener once had a row of broccoli plants. Only two had aphids on them and both were quite infested. The two plants were dug up and the gardener discovered the plants had experienced root damage during transplanting. The healthy broccoli, which had experienced uninterrupted growth, went untouched by the insects, while nature eliminated the unhealthy plants. When transplanting, it is important to handle the seedlings gently, and to touch them as little as possible. Plants do not like their bodies to be handled, though they do like human companionship and to have dead leaves removed from their stems. You should hold them only by the tips of their leaves (if the plant must be touched) or by the soil around their roots. If the seedlings have been grown in flats, use a hand fork to gently separate a 4 square-inch section of soil and plants from the rest. Using the fork, gently lift the section from the flat and place it on the ground. Then carefully pull away one plant at a time from the section for transplanting. If the day is particularly dry, hot or windy, the section should be placed on a wet towel and three of its sides should be protected from exposure by the towel. Always keep as much soil around the roots as possible. If the seedling has been grown in a pot, turn the pot upside down, letting the plant stem pass between your second and third fingers, and tap firmly on the bottom of the pot with your other hand. Or tap the lip of the pot on something solid.

In all cases, if the plants are root bound (roots so tightly grown together that with the soil they constitute a tight mass), gently spread the roots out in all directions. This process is important, because the plant would spend critical growth energy in sending out a new, wide-ranging root system for eating and drinking, when a good root system has already been produced. How much better if the energy goes into the natural flow of continuous growth rather than into the correction of an abnormal situation. In spreading the roots out, we physically minimize a problem which has occurred when the plant was kept in a starting flat or pot too long.

Be sure to place the seedling into a large enough hole so that the plant can be buried up to its first set of true leaves. This way, as the soil is packed down under the pressure of watering, the final soil level will remain high enough to cover the upper roots. Press the soil firmly around the seedling, but not too tightly. Tight packing will damage the roots and will not allow the proper penetration of water, nutriments and air. Too loose a soil will allow air and moisture to concentrate around the roots. This will cause root burn and decay. Firm contact of the plant's roots with the soil is necessary for the proper absorption of water and nutriment by the plant through the roots. Water the seedlings after transplanting to help settle the soil around the roots, to eliminate excess air spaces and to provide an adequate amount of water for growth.

A second reason for transplanting seedlings up to their first two leaves is to prevent them from becoming top-heavy and bending over during the early growth period. If the plant bends over, it will upright itself, but a very tough neck will be created that will reduce the quality and size of the plant and vegetable. Onions and garlic, however, do better if the bulb will not have so much weight to push against.

Transplanting should be used whenever possible (see transplanting information later in this section). Space and water are conserved in this way, because seedlings in flats require less of both. More importantly, transplanting is a way to improve plant health. Beds become compacted as they are watered from day to day. Thus, if a seed is planted directly in the bed, some compaction will have occurred by the time it is a "child" a month later and, in some cases, so much so after two months when it is likely to be an "adolescent", that its "adulthood" may be seriously affected. If, instead, you transplant the one-month old "child" into the growing bed, a strong adult root system can develop during the next two months and a good adult life is likely. In fact, a study at the University of California at Berkeley in the 1950's indicated that a 2-4% increase in root health can increase yields 2 to 4 times.[18]

Planting by the Phases of the Moon

One of the most controversial aspects of the biodynamic/ French intensive method is the planting of seeds and the transplanting of seedlings by phases of the moon. *Short and extra-long germinating seeds* are planted *two days before the New*

Most vegetables should be transplanted up to their first two leaves.

proper

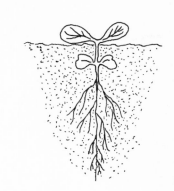

improper

result

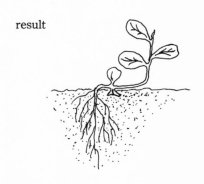

18. Charles Morrow Wilson, *Roots: Miracles Below—The Web of Life Beneath Our Feet,* Doubleday and Company, Garden City, New York, 1968, p. 105.

PLANTING BY THE PHASES OF THE MOON

2 days before New Moon

Plant short and extra-long germinating seeds (most vegetables and herbs) into flats and/or beds

First 7 days

Balanced increase in rate of root and leaf growth

Moonlight +
Lunar Gravity –

Second 7 days

Increased leaf growth rate

Moonlight +
Lunar gravity +

KEY:

● New Moon
◐ First Quarter
○ Full Moon
◑ Fourth Quarter
 + = Increasing
 – = Decreasing

Moon, when the first significant magnetic forces occur, and up to seven days after the New Moon. *Long germinating seeds* are planted *at the Full Moon* and up to seven days afterward. *Seedlings* are *transplanted at the same time.* Both planting periods take advantage of the full sum of the forces of nature, including gravity, light and magnetism. The greatest sum of increasing forces occurs at the New Moon. The lunar gravitational pull which produces high tides in the oceans and water tides in the soil is very high. And the moon, which is dark, gets progressively lighter. (See drawing.) The importance of the time of the month in planting seeds and transplanting is not so much in the exact day on which you perform the task, but rather in generally taking advantage of the impetus provided by nature.

By placing short germinating seeds in the ground two days before the lunar tide forces are greatest, the seed has time to absorb water. The force exerted on the water in the seed helps create a "tide" that helps burst the seed coat in conjunction with the forces produced by the swelling of the seed. No doubt you have wondered why one time beet seeds come up almost immediately and another time the germinating process takes two weeks in the same bed under similar conditions. Temperature and moisture differences, pH changes and humus levels may influence the seeds in each case. but the next time you note marked difference in germination time, check your calendar to determine the phase the moon was in when the seeds were sown. You may be surprised to find the moon had an influence.

Looking at the drawing, you can see that there are both increasing and decreasing lunar gravitational and light force influences that recur periodically during the lunar month. Sometimes the forces work against each other and sometimes they reinforce one another. When the lunar gravitational pull decreases and the amount of moonlight increases during *the first 7 days,* plants undergo a period of balanced growth. The decreasing lunar gravity (and the corresponding relative increase in the earth's gravity) *stimulates root growth.* At the same time, the increasing amount of moonlight *stimulates leaf growth.*

During *the second 7 days,* the lunar gravitational force reverses its relative direction and increases. This pull *slows down*

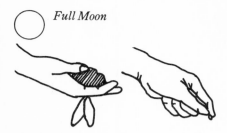

Full Moon

Transplant seedlings from flat into beds and plant long-germinating seeds (most flowers) into flats and/or beds

Third 7 days

Increased root growth rate

Moonlight –
Lunar gravity –

Fourth 7 days

Balanced decrease in rate of root and leaf growth (resting period)

Moonlight –
Lunar gravity +

the root growth as the earth's relative gravitational pull is lessened. The moonlight, on the other hand, continues to a peak and *leaf growth is especially stimulated.* If root growth has been sufficient during previous periods, then the proper amounts of nutriment and water will be conveyed to the above ground part of the plant and balanced, uninterruped growth will occur. In this time of increasing gravitational, moonlight and magnetic forces, seeds which have not yet germinated receive a special boost from nature. If they did not germinate at the time of the New Moon, they should do so by the Full Moon. It is during this period that Alan Chadwick says seeds cannot resist coming up and in which mushrooms suddenly appear overnight.

During *the third seven days,* the amount of moonlight decreases along with the lunar gravitational pull. As the moonlight decreases, the above ground *leaf growth slows down.* The *root growth is stimulated* again, however, as the lunar gravitational pull decreases. This is a good time to transplant, since the root growth is active. The activity enables the plant to better overcome root shock and promotes the development of a good root system while leaf growth has been slowed down. Then, 21 days later, when leaf growth is at a maximum, there will be a developed root system that can provide the plant with sufficient nutriment and water. It is also the time to plant long germinating seeds. Seeds which take approximately two weeks to germinate will then be in a state which can take advantage of the boost from the high gravitational pull of the New Moon.

During *the last 7 days,* the lunar gravitational force increases and *root growth slows down.* The amount of moonlight also decreases and *slows down leaf growth.* This period is one of a balanced decrease in growth or a period of rest, just as the first 7 days in the lunar month is a period of a balanced increase in growth. The last 7 days, then, is a rest period which comes before the bursting forth of a period of new life. Short and extra-long germinating seeds are planted two days before the New Moon so they will be able to take advantage of this time of new life. (The extra-long germinating seeds take approximately one month to germinate.) The short, long and extra-long germinating seed varieties are given in the large chart later in this section.

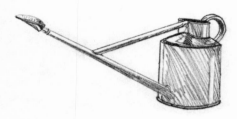

Haws watering can

Close-up of special upward pointing Haws watering rose.

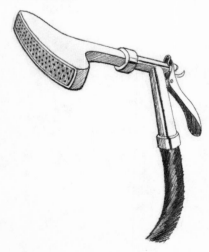

Ross watering fan attached to a variable water pressure gun.

In time, a planted seed bursts its seed coat around the twenty-eighth day of the lunar month and proceeds into a period of slow, balanced and increasing growth above and below ground, passes into a period of stimulated leaf growth, then goes into period of stimulated root growth (getting ready for the next period of stimulated leaf growth) and then goes into a time of rest. This plant growth cycle repeats itself monthly. Plants are transplanted at the Full Moon, so they may begin their life in the growth bed during a time of stimulated root growth. The stimulation is important to the plant because root shock occurs during transplanting. It is also important for the plant's root system to be well developed, so it can later provide the leaves, flowers and vegetables with water and nutriment. The transplanted plant then enters into a time of rest before beginning another monthly cycle. The workings of nature are beautiful.

(It should be noted that planting by the phases of the moon is a nuance which improves the health and quality of plants. If you do not follow the moon cycles, your plants will still grow satisfactorily. However, as your soil improves and as you gain experience, the nuances will become more important and will have a greater effect. Try it and see.)

Watering

The watering of beds and flats in the biodynamic/French intensive method is performed in a way which approximates rainfall as much as possible. The fine rain also absorbs beneficial air borne nutriments, as well as air, which help the growth process. For seeds and seedlings in flats, a special English Haws sprinkling can[19] is used, which has fine holes in the sprinkler's "rose". The "rose" points up so that when you water, the shower first goes up into the air where much of the pressure built up (when the water is forced through the rose) is dissipated. The water then falls on the plants from above like rain with only the force of gravity pulling the water down. When watering planting beds, the same method of shooting the water into the air and letting it fall back down may be used, using a water gun with a fan spray nozzle[20] attached to the gun. Or, the fan may be used without the water gun. (If a gun is used, a heavy duty hose will be required to contain the water pressure.) This method of shooting water into the air in a relatively fine rain means the soil in the bed will pack down less and that the plants will not be hit and damaged by a hard water spray. If you choose to point the fan downward, stand as far away from the plants as possible and/or keep the water pressure adjusted to a low point so soil compaction and water damage problems will be minimized.

19. Available by mail order from: Walter F. Nicke, Box 667G, Hudson, N.Y. 12534.

20. A Ross No. 20 is the best one.

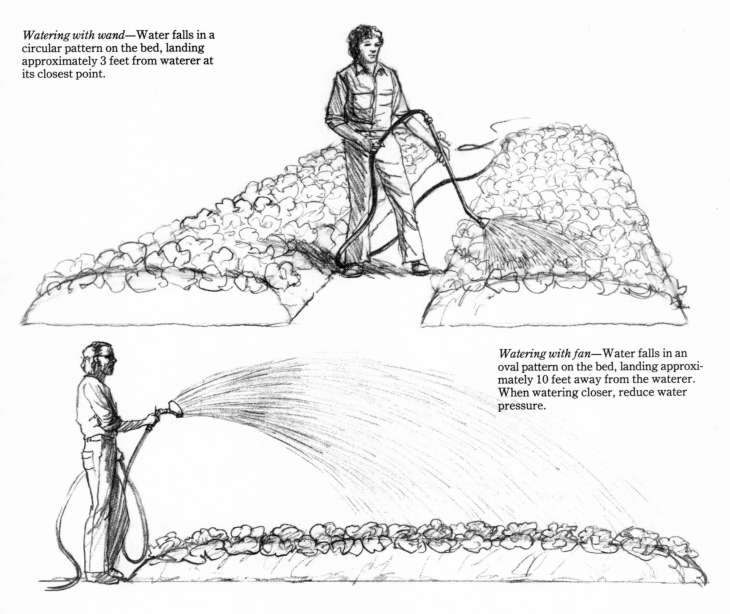

Watering with wand—Water falls in a circular pattern on the bed, landing approximately 3 feet from waterer at its closest point.

Watering with fan—Water falls in an oval pattern on the bed, landing approximately 10 feet away from the waterer. When watering closer, reduce water pressure.

Daily watering also washes the dust, grime and insects from plant leaves and creates a deliciously moist atmosphere conducive to good plant growth and thriving microbiotic life.

Some plants, such as those of the cabbage family, like to have wet leaves. It is all right, and in fact beneficial, to water these plants from overhead. Other plants, such as tomatoes, peas and members of the squash and melon families, can suffer from wilt, mildew and the rotting of their fruit when their leaves are wet, especially in foggy or humid climates. Care should normally be taken, when watering these plants, to water only the soil whenever possible. (In drier climates it will probably not matter.) To do this, the fan should be pointed sideways. A better method is to use a watering wand which will allow you to more easily place water under the plant's leaves.

Technique for watering tomato plants using wand.

18"

2 ft.

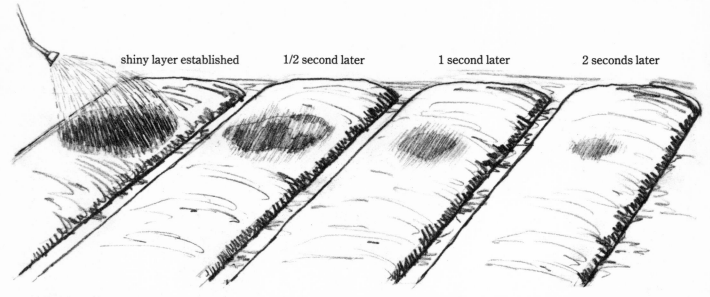

shiny layer established   1/2 second later   1 second later   2 seconds later

A newly prepared bed is properly watered when the *shiny layer* of excess water disappears within 1/2 to 3 seconds after watering stops.

The beds are watered lightly each day to keep them evenly moist. (Watering may be more or less frequent when the weather is warmer or cooler than normal.)

Mature plants in beds should be watered when the heat of the day first subsides. This is about two hours before sunset during the summer and earlier during the winter. However, weather conditions, especially cloud cover, may necessitate earlier watering. The cool water is warmed by the warm soil and the water temperature is modified by the time it reaches the plant roots. The roots suffer less shock and the soil and plants have more time to absorb water during the cooler, less windy night. The availability of moisture is critical, since plants do a significant amount of their growing at night. If you water early in the morning, much of the water will be lost in evaporation caused by the sun and wind and the watering will be less effective. The loss will be even greater if you water at mid-day. If you water in the evening, the plants will be more susceptible to mildew and rust problems due to unevaporated water left on their leaves. By watering primarily in the late afternoon, you allow the water to percolate into the soil for a half day or more before the sun and wind reappear in strength. When they do, the bed will be a good reservoir of water from which the plants can draw.

Seeds and seedlings in flats and seeds and immature plants in the growing beds may have to be watered in the morning and at noon as well as late in the afternoon. Until the living mulch effect occurs, the flats and beds need more watering because they dry out more rapidly. As the leaves grow closer together, less watering will be required.

To determine how much water to give a bed each day, strive for a 1/2 to 15 second "shiny".[21] When you first begin to water, a *shiny layer* of excess water will appear on top of the

21. Another simple way to estimate the amount of water a bed is receiving is to first measure the gallons per minute. Turn the hose on and point the spray into a 1 gallon jar or 4 qt. watering can. If, for example, it takes 15 seconds to fill the jar then you know you are delivering 4 gallons per minute to the bed. Currently, in our moderately heavy clay, we find each 5' × 20' bed will take anywhere from 5-20 gallons daily (10 gallons on the average) depending on the weather, the size of the plants, the type of plant and the tightness of the soil.

soil. If you stop watering immediately, the shiny layer will disappear quickly. You should water, then, until the shiny layer remains for 1/2 to 15 seconds after you have stopped watering. The actual time involved will differ depending on the texture of your soil. The more clayey the texture, the shorter the time will be. A newly prepared bed with good texture and structure will probably have enough water when a 1/2 to 3 second "shiny" is reached. A newly prepared clayey bed may indicate enough watering has been done with a 3 to 5 second "shiny", since a clayey soil both retains more moisture *and* lets the water in less rapidly. A month old bed (which has compacted somewhat due to the watering process) may require a 5 to 8 second "shiny" and beds two to three months old may require a longer one.

Eventually, the watering process will become automatic and you will not even have to think about when the bed has received enough water. You will know intuitively when the point has been reached. Remember to allow for the different natures of plants. Squash plants, for instance, will want a lot of water in comparison to tomato plants. One way to determine if you have watered enough is to go out the next morning and poke your finger into the bed. If the soil is evenly moist for the first two inches and continues to be moist below this level, you are watering properly. If the soil is dry for part or all of the first two inches, you need more "shiny". If the soil is soggy in part or all of the upper two inches, you need less "shiny".

Remember also to adjust your watering according to the weather. A bed may lose more moisture on a cloudy, windy, *dry* day than on a hot, clear, *humid* and still one. And there are times when the flats and beds need no water or watering twice a day. It is important to note these differences and to become sensitive to the needs of the plants. You should water for good fruit, flower and vegetable production, not just so the plant will stay alive. Be sure to water the sides and edges of the planting beds more. These areas, which many people miss or under-emphasize, are critical because they are subject to more evaporation than the middle of the bed. Pay special attention to older beds. The soil tends to compact in older beds, so two light waterings may be required to get the proper penetration. Similarly, newly dug but still unplanted beds should be watered daily so they will not lose their moisture content. A transplant in a bed which has a low moisture level (except in the recently watered upper 2 inches) will have difficulty growing well. If you wait until plants are wilting and drooping to water, the plants will revive but they will have suffered some permanent damage—an open invitation for pests and diseases. Slight drooping, however, is not usually a sign you should water. Plants are just minimizing the water loss (due to transpiration) when they droop on a hot day and watering them at this time will increase water loss rather than lessen it. It will also weaken the plant through too much pampering.

Weeding

Weeding is not required as often as in other gardening methods due to the living mulch provided by the plants. Usually, weeding needs to be performed only once, about a month after the bed is planted. A bed prepared in a new area may have to be weeded more often at first, however, since many dormant seeds will be raised to a place in the soil where they can germinate readily. Over a period of time, as the soil becomes richer and more alive, you will probably have fewer weeds, since they tend to thrive more in poor and deficient soils rather than in healthy ones.

There really is no such thing as a "weed". A weed is just a plant which is growing in an area where you, the gardener, do not want it to grow. In fact, many so called weeds, such as stinging nettle, are quite beneficial to the soil and other plants. (This will be discussed in more detail in the section on Companion Planting.) Instead of weeding indiscriminately, the natures and uses of the different weeds should be learned so you will be able to identify and leave some of the most beneficial ones in the growing beds. The weeds taken out should be placed in the compost pile. They are rich in trace minerals and other nutriments, and will help grow good crops in the next season. And until taken out, the weeds help establish a faster, nourishing mini-climate for your current crops.

Weeds are generally heartier than cultivated plants since they are genetically closer to the parental plant stock and nearer to the origin of the plant species. They tend to germinate before cultivated plants. Usually you should wait to remove these plants from the beds until the cultured plants catch up with the weeds in height or until the cultured plants become established (about transplanting size)—whichever comes first. Weeding before this time is likely to disturb the germinating cultured plant seeds or to disturb the developing new plant root systems, causing interrupted plant growth and a weakened plant. Be sure to remove any grass plants which develop in the beds even after the first weeding. These plants put out incredibly large root systems which interfere with those of other plants in their competition for nutriments and water.

Planting in Season

Vegetables, flowers and herbs—all plants for that matter—should be planted in season. This is a good way to love your plants. If they are forced (grown out of season), much of their energy is used up straining to combat unseasonable weather in the form of cold, heat, rain or drought. Less energy is left for balanced growth, and a plant with limited reserves of energy is more susceptible to disease and insect attack. Plants are not unlike people.

Correct posture for easy weeding.

SATISFACTORY (AND OPTIMAL) PLANT GROWING TEMPERATURE RANGES[22]
Determine Planting Range Calendar For Your Own Area

Crop Season	Temp. Range	Optimal Temp. Range	Plant
Cool Season Crops	30 °F.		Asparagus • Rhubarb
	45-85 °F.	(55-75 °F.)	Chicory • Chive • Garlic • Leek • Onion • Salsify • Shallot
	40-75 °F.	(60-65 °F.)	Beet • Broad Bean • Broccoli • Brussels Sprouts • Cabbage • Chard • Collard • Horseradish • Kale • Kohlrabi • Parsnip • Radish • Rutabaga • Sorrel • Spinach • Turnip
	45-75 °F.	(60-65 °F.)	Artichoke • Carrot • Cauliflower • Celeriac • Celery • Chicory • Chinese Cabbage • Endive • Florence Fennel • Lettuce • Mustard • Parsley • Pea • Potato
Warm Season Crops	50-80 °F.	(60-70 °F.)	Bean • Lima Bean
	50-95 °F.	(60-75 °F.)	Corn • Cowpea • New Zealand Spinach
	50-90 °F.	(65-75 °F.)	Pumpkin • Squash
	60-90 °F.	(65-75 °F.)	Cucumber • Muskmelon
Hot Season Crops	65-80 °F.	(70-75 °F.)	Sweet Pepper • Tomato
	65-95 °F.	(70-85 °F.)	Eggplant • Hot Pepper • Okra • Sweet Potato • Watermelon

22. From James Edward Knott, *Handbook for Vegetable Growers,* John Wiley & Sons, Inc., New York, 1957, pp. 6-7.

SOIL TEMPERATURE CONDITIONS FOR VEGETABLE SEED GERMINATION[23]

CROP	Minimum, °F.	Optimum Range, °F.	Optimum, °F.	Maximum, °F.
Asparagus	50	60-85	75	95
Bean	60	60-85	80	95
Bean, Lima	60	65-85	85	85
Beet	40	50-85	85	95
Cabbage	40	45-95	85	100
Carrot	40	45-85	80	95
Cauliflower	40	45-85	80	100
Celery	40	60-70	70*	85*
Chard, Swiss	40	50-85	85	95
Corn	50	60-95	95	105
Cucumber	60	60-95	95	105
Eggplant	60	75-90	85	95
Lettuce	35	40-80	75	85
Muskmelon	60	75-95	90	100
Okra	60	70-95	95	105
Onion	35	50-95	75	95
Parsley	40	50-85	75	90
Parsnip	35	50-70	65	85
Pea	40	40-75	75	85
Pepper	60	65-95	85	95
Pumpkin	60	70-90	95	100
Radish	40	45-90	85	95
Spinach	35	45-75	70	85
Squash	60	70-95	95	100
Tomato	50	60-85	85	95
Turnip	40	60-105	85	105
Watermelon	60	70-95	95	105

*Daily fluctuation to 60° or lower at night is essential.

23. From James Edward Knott, *Handbook for Vegetable Growers*, John Wiley & Sons, Inc., New York, 1957, p. 8.

The large planning charts which follow should be helpful. They are in great part based on our experience. They are generally complete and accurate. As testing continues the information will be revised and the chance of error reduced. It should be noted that

- Maximum yields may not be reached in the first year. Also, one plant, grown alone, will probably not produce as large a yield as one plant grown among several under mini-climate conditions.

- Seeds grown out of season will take longer to germinate and/or may decompose before they do unless grown under special greenhouse conditions.

- Closer spacing may be needed during the winter to make up for the slower plant growth during this period and to create a balanced winter mini-climate. (Try 3/4 or 1/2 the spacing distance with lettuce.) Closer spacing is sometimes also used to promote faster, balanced growth due to a more rapidly reached mini-climate. Extra plants are thinned to make room for larger plants. Baby carrots and beets are a delicacy!

	PLANT	SEED			YIELD		
	A Plant	**B** Approx. Seeds/Ounce[24]	**C** Minimum Legal Germination Rate[25]	**D** Ounces Seed/100 Sq. Ft. (Adj. for Germ. Rate and Curv. Surf.)[26]	**E** Possible B/FIM Pounds Yield/100 Sq. Ft.[27]	**F** Possible B/FIM Pounds Yield/Plant[28]	**G** Avg. U.S. Pounds Yield/100 Sq. Ft.[29]
1	Artichoke, Jerusalem	Sprouted 2 oz. tuber pieces	—, R	9.6 lbs.	100-206-420+	1.3-5.4+	D
2	Artichoke, Regular	From divided roots	D	2.6 roots	D	D	16.5
3	Asparagus	700	.70	.24 or 120 roots	9.5-19-38	.08-.3	5
4	Beans, Broad	20-70	.70R	19.2-5.5	5-9-18	.02-.06	D
5	Beans, Lima, Bush	20-70	.70R	34.3-9.8	11.5-17.2-23 Dry	.024-.048	5.7+
6	Beans, Lima, PoleN	20-70	.70R	19.3-5.5	11.5+-17.2+-23+ Dry	.042+-.085+	5.7+
7	Beans, Snap, Bush	100	.75R	14.4	30-72-108	.027-.1	8.2
8	Beans, Snap, PoleN	100	.75R	6.4	30+-72+-108+	.062+-.225+	8.2+
9	Beets, Cylindra	1,600	.65R	1.8	110-220-540	.056-.28	D
10	Beets, Regular	1,600	.65R	1.8	55-110-270	.028-.14	30
11	Broccoli	9,000	.75	.01	26-39-53	.33-.68	17.4
12	Brussels Sprouts	8,500	.70	.01	71-106-142	1.6-3.2	23.4
13	Cabbage, Chinese	9,500	.75	.03	96-191-383	.55-2.2	D
14	Cabbage, Regular	8,500	.75	.01	96-191-383	1.2-4.9	45
15	Carrots	23,000	.55##	.34	100-150-1,080	.02-.25	58.9
16	Cauliflower	10,000	.75	.01	44-100-291	.57-3.7	23
17	Celery	70,000	.55	.01	240-480-959+	.5-2.0	110
18	Chard	1,200	.65R	.35	200-405-810	.74-3.0	D
19	Collards	8,000	.80	.02	96-191-383	.8-3.2	D
20	Corn	100-200	.75	.6-.3 / .7-.35	17-34-68 Shelled, Wet	.22-.88 / .4-1.5	15.3
21	Cucumbers	1,000	.80	.15	158-316-581	1.3-4.8	20.6
22	Eggplant	6,000	.60	.01	54-108-163	1.2-3.7	35.6
23	Garlic	12zz	.5zz	20 lbs.	60-120-240+	.03-.125+	32
24	Horseradish	Live roots used	—	120 roots	D	D	D
25	Kale	10,000	.75	.01	76-114-153	1.0-2.0	16.0
26	Kohlrabi	8,000	.75	.2	67-135-270	.06-.25	D
27	Leeks	11,000	.60	.3	240-480-960	.13-.5	D
28	Lettuce, Head	25,000	.80	.01	75-150-300	1.0-2.85	48.6
29	Lettuce, Leaf	25,000	.80	.02	135-202-540	.5-2.0	48.6

✱ H	I	J	K	L	M	N	O	P	Q	R	S	
In BED Spacing In Inches	Plants/100 Sq. Ft.[30]	Short/Long/Extra-Long Germ. Rate	Plant Initially In Flats/Beds	In FLATS Spacing in Inches[31]	Approx. Plants/Flat (Adj. for Germ. Rate)[31][32]	Approx. Time In Flats-In Weeks[31][33]	Approx. Weeks to Maturity	Harvesting Period In Weeks—Up To:	Remarks and Especially Good Varieties	Pounds Eaten/Year[34] Avg. Person in U.S.	Approx. Max. Pounds Seed Yield/100 Sq. Ft.[40]	Heavy Giver (HG), Light Feeder (LF), Low Nitrogen User (LNU), Heavy Feeder (HF)
15	77	L	F	2 / —	60 / —	4 / —	17-26	—	41	D	420+	HF
72	2.6	L	B	—	—	—	D, P	8	—	D	D	HF
12	120	L	Seeds in F	1 / 2	175 / 60	D	4 Yrs./Seeds 1 Yr./Roots	8	—	1.2	8.7	HF
8	270	S	B	—	—	—	11	8	Fava Beans	D	18.0	HG
6	480	S	B	—	—	—	9-11	12	—	} 1.3	17.8	HG
8	270	S	B	—	—	—	11-13	12	—		22.3	HG
4	1,080	S	B	—	—	—	8	12	—	} 8.5	17.0	HG
6	480	S	B	—	—	—	8-9	12	—		29.7	HG
3	1,920	S	B	—	—	—	8-9	—	Twice the Weight	} 1.9	30.6	LF
3	1,920	S	B	—	—	—	8-9	—	—		30.6	LF
15	77	S	F	1 / 2	187 / 60	4-6# 8-10 / 2-3	8-9	4-6	43	1.3	5.5	HF
18	44	S	F	1 / 2	175 / 60	4-6# 8-10 / 2-3	11-13	12	—	.3	2.8	HF
10	173	S	F	1 / 2	187 / 60	4-6# 8-10 / 2-3	7-11**	—	—	D	6.1	HF
15	77	S	F	1 / 2	187 / 60	4-6# 8-10 / 2-3	9-16**	—	—	10.7	3.6	HF
2	4,320	S	B	—	—	—	9-11	—	—	8.4	17.8	LF
15	77	S	F	1 / 2	187 / 60	4-6# 8-10 / 2-3	8-12**	—	—	1.3	1.0	HF
6	480	L	F	1 / 2	137 / 60	8-12# 14-16 / 6-8	15-19	—	—	7.5	9.9	HF
8	270	S	B	—	—	—	7-8	44	Burpee Fordhook	D	29.0	HF
12	120	S	F	1 / 2	200 / 60	4-6# 8-10 / 2-3	12	24	44	D	D	HF
15z / 18z	77 / 44	S	F	1 / —	187	2 / —	9-13**	—	—	14.0 Shelled Wet	10.3 / 7.1	HF
12	120	S	F	2 / —	48 / —	3-4 / —	7-10	26	—	3.1 Reg. 7.6 Pickle	4.1	HF
18	44	L	F	1 / 2	150 / 60	6-8# 12-14 / 4-6# 8-12	10-11	13	—	.5	.6	HF
3	1,920	L	F	1 / —	122 / —	4-6 / —	17-26	—	—	.3	240 (Bulbs)	LF
12	120	L	B	—	—	—	26	—	—	D	D	LF
15	77	S	F	1 / 2	187 / 60	4-6# 8-10 / 2-3	8-9	17	—	D	3.8	HF
4	1,080	S	F	1 / 2	187	4-6# 8-10	7-8	—	—	D	20.1	LF
3	1,920	S	F	1 / —	150	8-12	19	—	—	D	9.8	LF
12	120	S	F	1 / 2	200 / 60	2-3 / 1-2	11-13	—	—	} 22	1.2	HF
8	270	S	F	1 / 2	200 / 60	2-3 / 1-2	6-13**	—	—		2.0	HF

PLANT	FOOD NEEDED	MATERIALS NEEDED				
A *Plant*	**B** *Pounds You Select*	**C** *Approx. Number Plants You Need*[35]	**D** *Approx. Sq. Ft. You Need*[36]	**E** *Approx. Flats You Need*[37]	**F** *Approx. Ounces/Seed You Need*[38]	
1 Artichoke, Jerusalem						
2 Artichoke, Regular						
3 Asparagas						
4 Beans, Broad						
5 Beans, Lima, Bush						
6 Beans, Lima, Pole[N]						
7 Beans, Snap, Bush						
8 Beans, Pole[N]						
9 Beets, Cylindra						
10 Beets, Regular						
11 Broccoli						
12 Brussels Sprouts						
13 Cabbage, Chinese						
14 Cabbage, Regular						
15 Carrots						
16 Cauliflower						
17 Celery						
18 Chard						
19 Collards						
20 Corn						
21 Cucumbers						
22 Eggplant						
23 Garlic						
24 Horseradish						
25 Kale						
26 Kohlrabbi						
27 Leeks						
28 Lettuce, Head						
29 Lettuce, Leaf						

YIELDS	
G	**H**
Your Actual Yield/100 Sq. Ft.	*Your Yield Compared With U.S. Avg.*[39]

CODES

D — Do not know yet

R — Replant at points where germination fails. We call this "spotting".

P — Perennial

N — Use narrow bed: 2 feet wide

S — Short Germinating Seed (1-7 days)

L — Long Germinating Seed (8-21 days)

X — Extra-Long Germinating Seed (22-28 days)

B — In Beds

F — In Flats

— First set of figures: summer growing in lathhouse for fall set-out

Second set of figures: winter growing in greenhouse for spring set-out.

Harden off for 2 days outside in flat before transplanting into bed.

— Plant 2 seeds/center to compensate for low germination rate.

** — Depending on variety selected.

Z — 15 inch spacing for non-hybrids; 18 inch spacing for hybrids. Sequential information in columns D, F, H and I should be used according to spacing chosen

ZZ — Based on Ecology Action experience.

+ — Yield may be significantly higher.

-- — Not applicable.

FOOTNOTES

24. From James Edward Knott, *Handbook for Vegetable Growers*, John Wiley and Sons, Inc., New York, 1957, p. 17.

25. Ibid., pp. 192 and 193.

26. To determine amount, divide Column I by Column B by Column C.

27. Estimates based on our experience and research. Use lower figure if you are a beginning gardener; middle, if a good one; third, if an excellent one.

28. $E \div I$

29. U.S. Department of Agriculture, *Agricultural Statistics—1972*, U.S. Governmental Printing Office, Washington, D.C., pp. 151-188.

30. Curved surface adds about 20% to planting surface, so *120 plants* fit in 100 square feet on 12 inch (1 foot) centers, rather than 100 plants.

31. Upper part of box is for initial seeding in flat. Lower part is for later transplanted spacing in another flat, when that is recommended.

32. Assumes Flat with internal dimensions of 13 inches by 21 inches (or 273 square inches) in which at least 250 plants fit on 1 inch centers and 60 plants on 2 inch centers.

33. From James Edward Knott, *Handbook for Vegetables Growers*, John Wiley and Sons, Inc., New York, 1957, p. 14 and from our experience.

34. U.S. Department of Agriculture, *Agricultural Statistics—1972*, U.S. Governmental Printing Office, Washington, D.C., pp. 238, 239, 241, 242, 244, 245.

35. $S \div F$

36. $S \div E$. Use lower figure in E if you are a beginning gardener; middle, if a good one; third if an excellent one.

37. $T \div M$

38. $U \div D$

39. $X \div G$

40. Based in part on standard yield figures from James Edward Knott, *Handbook ofr Vegetable Growers*, John Wiley and Sons, Inc. New York, 1957, pp. 198-199 in combination with a multiplier factor based on our research and experience. The result, however, is preliminary, for your guidance, and is very experimental. Remember, if growing seed, to adjust for germination rate when determining amount to grow for your use.

41. Harvest after die-back of plants.

42. From James Edward Knott, *Handbook for Vegetable Growers*, John Wiley and Sons, Inc., New York, 1957, p. 14.

43. Can cut smaller heading secondary and tertiary side shoots also. In addition, leaves generally have twice the nutritive value of the "heads"!

44. Contains the same amount of general protein (not amino acids) and 50-100% more calcium per cup as milk, yet may produce up to 6 times the cups per unit of area!

PLANT	SEED			YIELD		
A	B	C	D	E	F	G
Plant	Approx. Seeds/Ounce[24]	Minimum Legal Germination Rate[25]	Ounces Seed/100 Sq. Ft. (Adj. for Germ. Rate and Curv. Surf.)[26]	Possible B/FIM Pounds Yield/100 Sq. Ft.[27]	Possible B/FIM Pounds Yield/Plant[28]	Avg. U.S. Pounds Yield/100 Sq. Ft.[29]
30 Melons	1,200	.75	.09	50-72-145	.6-1.9	20C / 36.5
31 Mustard	15,000	.75	.04	180-225-270	.37-.56	D
32 Okra	500	.50	.48	30-60-120	.25-1.0	D
33 Onions, Bunching	9,500	.70R	2.6	100-200-540	.006-.03	D
34 Onions, Regular	9,500	.70	.29	100-200-540	.05-.28	} 68.6
35 Onions, Torpedo	9,500	.70	.29	200-400-1,080	.1-.56	
36 Parsley	18,000	.60	.1	26-52-106	.025-.1	D
37 Parsnips	12,000	.60##	2.7	119-238-479	.06-.25	D
38 Peas, Bush	50-230	.80R	3 lbs.-10.4 oz.	25-53-106	.013-.055	} 6.8
39 Peas, PoleN	50-230	.80R	1 lb. 11 oz.-5.9 oz	25+-53+-106+	.023+-.1+	
40 Peppers, Cayenne	4,500	.55	.05	10-25-40	.08-.33	D
41 Peppers, Green	4,500	.55	.05	36-83-131	.3-1.1	18.8
42 Potatoes, Irish	47	—	20 lbs–26.75 lbs.	100-200-600	.47-2.8	52.6
43 Potatoes, Sweet	49	—	35.67 lbs-26.75 lbs.	82-164-492	.38-2.3	23.6
44 Pumpkin	110	.75	.23	48-96-191	2.5-10.0	D
45 Radishes	2,000	.75R	3.5	100-200-540	.006-.03	D
46 Rhubarb	1,700Y	.60Y	.03	D	D	D
47 Rutabagas	12,000	.75	.05	200-400-960	.4-2.0	D
48 Salsify	1,800	.75R	3.2	200-400-1,080	.046-.25	D
49 Spinach, New Zealand	350	.40	.86	180-225-270	1.5-2.25	D
50 Spinach, Regular	2,800	.60	.64	50-100-225	.046-.20	12.1
51 Squash, Crook Neck	300 (Bush)	.75	.34	35-75-150	.45-1.9	D
52 Squash, Patty Pan	300 (Bush)	.75	.34	75-150-307	1.0-4.0	D
53 Squash, Winter	100 (Vine)	.75	.25	50-100-191	2.6-10.0	D
54 Squash, Zucchini	300 (Bush)	.75	.24	160-319-478+	3.0-9.0	D
55 Sunflowers	650 (In Shell)Y	.50+Y	.09	D	D	D
56 Tomatoes	11,000	.75	.004/.005/.007	100-194-418	1.9-13.9	30.7
57 Turnips	13,000	.80R	.18	100-200-360	.05-.19	D
58 Watermelon	225-300	.70	.76-.57/.27-.21/ .25-.19/.19-.14	50-100-320	.41-10.6	24.3

BEDS/FLATS							MATURITY		RE-MARKS	FOOD NEEDED	SEED YIELD	
H * In BED Spacing In Inches	I Plants/100 Sq. Ft.[30]	J Short/Long/Extra-Long Germ. Rate	K Plant Initially In Flats/Beds	L In FLATS Spacing in Inches[31]	M Approx. Plants/Flat (Adj. for Germ. Rate)[31][32]	N Approx. Time In Flats-In Weeks[31][33]	O Approx. Weeks to Maturity	P Harvesting Period In Weeks—Up To:	Q Remarks and Especially Good Varieties	R Pounds Eaten/Year[34] Avg. Person in U.S.	S Approx. Max. Pounds Seed Yield/100 Sq. Ft.[40]	Heavy Giver (HG), Light Feeder (LF), Low Nitrogen User (LNU), Heavy Feeder (HF)
15	77	S	F	2 / —	45 / —	3-4 / —	12-17**	13	45	7.8c	2.9	HF
6	480	S	F	1 / —	187 / —	3-4 / —	5-6	8	—	D	5.7	HF
12	120	L	F	1 / 2	125 / 60	6-8 / 3-4	7-8	13	—	D	9.3	HF
1	17,280	S	B	—	—	—	17	—	—	D	39.6	LF
3	1,920	S	F	1 / —	175 / —	10-12# 12-14 / —	14-17	—	—	} 1.2	10.3	LF
3	1,910	S	F	1 / —	175 / —	10-12# 12-14 / —	14-17	—	46	}	10.3	LF
4	1,080	L	F	1 / 2	150 / 60	8-12 / 6-8	10-13	40	—	D	24.8	HF
3	1,920	L	B	—	—	—	15	—	—	D	24.8	LF
3	1,920	S	B	—	—	—	8-10	12	—	} 5.9	21.6	HG
4	1,080	S	B	—	—	—	10-11	12	—	}	12.1	HG
12	120	L	F	1 / 2	137 / 60	6-8# 12-14 / 4-6	9-11	17	—	D	.1	HF
12	120	L	F	1 / 2	137 / 60	6-8# 12-14 / 4-6	9-12	17	—	2.5	.3	HF/LNU
centers depth	214	L	In dark place	—	—	—	17	—	48	133.4	200-600	LF
centers depth	214	L	F	3 / —	30 / —	3-4 / —	26-34	—	—	6.2	492	LF/LNU
30	19	S	F	2 / —	45 / —	3-4 / —	14-16	—	50	.6	5.1	HF
2	4320	S	F	—	—	—	3-9**	—	51	D	20.6	LF
24	30	L	F	1 / 2	150 / 60	D / D	3 Years Roots 1 Yr.	D	52	.03	D	HF
6	480	S	F	1 / —	187 / —	3-4 / —	13	—	—	D	5.4	LF
2	4,320	S	B	—	—	—	17	—	—	D	27.7	LF
12	120	L	F	2 / —	24 / —	3-4 / —	10	42	Drought Resistant	D	17.2	HF
4	1,080	S	F	1 / —	150 / —	3-4 / —	6-7	—	—	1.8	10.8	HF
15	77	S	F	2 / —	45 / —	3-4 / —	10	17+	—	D	6.1	HF
15	77	S	F	2 / —	45 / —	3-4 / —	7	17+	—	D	6.1	HF
30	19	S	F	2 / —	45 / —	3-4 / —	11-17**	17+	—	D	5.7	HF
18	53	S	F	2 / —	45 / —	3-4 / —	7-9	26	Burpee's Fordhook	D	6.1	HF
24	30	S	F	1 / 2	100+ / 60	2-3 / 1-2	12	—	—	D	D	HF
18/21 /24T	53/39 /39	S	F	1 / 2	187 / 60	6-8# 12-14 / 3-4	8-13	17+	—	31.1	5.5	HF
3	1,920	S	F	—	—	—	5-10**	—	—	D	14.7	LF/LNU
12/18/ 21/24W	120/44 /39/30	S	F	2 / —	42 / —	3-4 / —	10-13	13	53	13.9	2.6	HF

PLANT	FOOD NEEDED	MATERIALS NEEDED				
A *Plant*	B *Pounds You Select*	C *Approx. Number Plants You Need*[35]	D *Approx. Sq. Ft. You Need*[36]	E *Approx. Flats You Need*[37]	F *Approx. Ounces/Seed You Need*[38]	
30 Melons						
31 Mustard						
32 Okra						
33 Onion, Bunching						
34 Onions, Regular						
35 Onions, Torpedo						
36 Parsley						
37 Parsnips						
38 Peas, Bush						
39 Peas, Pole[N]						
40 Peppers, Cayenne						
41 Peppers, Green						
42 Potatoes, Irish						
43 Potatoes, Sweet						
44 Pumpkin						
45 Radishes						
46 Rhubarb						
47 Rutabagas						
48 Salsify						
49 Spinach, New Zealand						
50 Spinach, Regular						
51 Squash, Crook Neck						
52 Squash, Patty Pan						
53 Squash, Winter						
54 Squash, Zucchini						
55 Sunflowers						
56 Tomatoes						
57 Turnips						
58 Watermelon						

YIELDS

G	H
Your Actual Yield/100 Sq. Ft.	*Your Yield Compared With U.S. Avg.*[39]

CODES

C — Cantaloupe

H — Honeydew

T — 18 inches for cherry tomatoes; 21 inches for regular tomatoes; 24 inches for large tomatoes. Sequential information in columns D, F, H and I should be used according to spacing chosen.

Y — Estimate

V — Approximate minimum

-- — Not applicable

W — 12 inches for midget varieties; remaining spacings experimental for regular varieties. Sequential information in columns D, F, H and I should be used according to spacing chosen.

— Plant 2 seeds/center to compensate for low germination rate.

R — Replant at points where germination fails. We call this "spotting".

D — Do not know yet.

S — Short Germinating Seed (1-7 days).

L — Long Germinating Seed (8-21 days).

X — Extra-Long Germinating Seed (22-28 days).

B — In Beds.

F — In Flats.

— First set of figures: summer growing in lathhouse for fall set-out

Second set of figures: winter growing in greenhouse for spring set-out

Harden off for 2 days outside in flat before transplanting into bed.

** — Depending on variety selected.

+ — Yield may be significantly higher.

FOOTNOTES

24. From James Edward Knott, *Handbook for Vegetable Growers*, John Wiley and Sons, Inc., New York, 1957, p. 17.

25. Ibid., pp. 192 and 193.

26. To determine amount, divide Column I by Column B by Column C.

27. Estimates based on our experience and research. Use lower figure if you are a beginning gardener; middle, if a good one; third, if an excellent one.

28. $E \div I$

29. U.S. Department of Agriculture, *Agricultural Statistics—1972*, U.S. Governmental Printing Office, Washington, D.C., pp. 151-188.

30. Curved surface adds about 20% to planting surface, so *120 plants* fit in 100 square feet on 12 inch (1 foot) centers, rather than 100 plants.

31. Upper part of box is for initial seeding in flat. Lower part is for later transplanted spacing in another flat, when that is recommended.

32. Assumes flat with internal dimensions of 13 inches by 21 inches (or 273 square inches) in which at least 250 plants fit on 1 inch centers and 60 plants on 2 inch centers.

33. From James Edward Knott, *Handbook for Vegetable Growers*, John Wiley and Sons, Inc., New York, 1957, p. 14 and from our experience.

34. U.S. Department of Agriculture, *Agricultural Statistics—1972*, U.S. Governmental Printing Office, Washington, D.C., pp. 238, 239, 241, 242, 244, 245.

35. $S \div F$

36. $S \div E$. Use lower figure in E if you are a beginning gardener; middle, if a good one; third, if and excellent one.

37. $T \div M$

38. $U \div D$

39. $X \div G$

40. Based in part on standard yield figures from James Edward Knott, *Handbook for Vegetable Growers,* John Wiley and Sons, Inc, New York, 1957, pp. 198-199 in combination with a multiplier factor based on our research and experience. The result, however, is preliminary, for your guidance, and is very experimental. Remember, if growing seed, to adjust for germination rate when determining amount to grow for your use.

45. Use French variety (Vilmorin's Cantalun—orange fleshed) or Israeli variety (Haogen—green fleshed). Both have smooth exterior without netting. This minimizes rotting.

46. Try the Torpedo onion. Its long shape is particularly suited to intensive raised bed gardening and farming, and it can produce twice the yield per unit of area.

47. 1.5—2.0 ounce pieces of slightly sprouted tubers use only 1 or 2 eyes left on potato piece.

48. Red "Lasoda" variety recommended. Note that stems and leaves are poisonous, as is any part of the tuber which has turned green. Get "seed" potatoes. Many in stores have been treated to retard sprouting.

49. Stem and root sections nicked in one piece from one end of sprouted tuber. About 3 to 4 of these "starts" will be obtained from each 8 ounce potato started in a flat. Get "seed" potatoes. Many in stores have been treated to retard sprouting.

50. Burpee's Triple Treat variety with hull-less seeds. No shelling of nutritious and tasty seeds!

51. Burpee's Sparkler variety: red top with white bottom half. Good looking.

52. Green parts poisonous.

53. Burpee's New Hampshire Midget variety

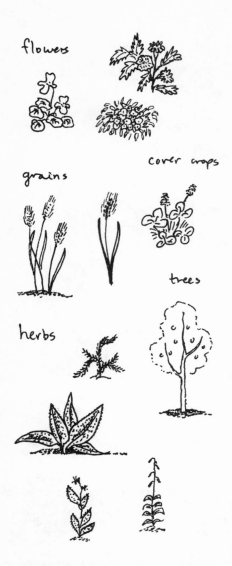

flowers

cover crops

grains

trees

herbs

The following spacings for grains, fibers, bush and dwarf fruit trees, berries and grapes, and cover crops are being tested at our research site. Increasingly many people want to grow them. They are fun to try. One hundred square feet of grain may yield 4, 8, 12 or more pounds of edible seed. Dwarf fruit trees, if nurtured properly can yield 50 to 100 pounds of fruit annually at maturity. Two trees on 8 foot centers in 100 square feet can yield 200 pounds together and the average person in the United States eats only about 162 pounds of tree fruit. Fava beans will probably yield the greatest amount of organic matter for you. Alfalfa and clover are also fun to use. Try medium red clover. It can be cut up to three times before it is dug in and has beautiful red flowers.

Our goal with wheat is to eventually get two 26 pound crops in an 8 month period. This would make possible one, 1 pound loaf of bread for every week in the year from 100 square feet! Then we could literally raise our own bread in our back-yards. Wheat can be threshed easily with a mini-thresher[54] made available by a public organization in your area. Sound impossible? Yields close to this are already occuring in some parts of the world. Our highest wheat yield to date is at the rate of about 12 pounds per 100 square foot bed using only 8 inches of water for the whole season and just compost we grew ourselves for fertilizer. The Zulus in South Africa use a technique similar to the biodynamic/French intensive method and grow grains with natural rainfall. See what you can do! Let us know if you get to 16 pounds to 26 pounds first—and how you do it.

54. One good foot-treadle powered model is available from CeCe Co., P.O. Box 8, Ibaraki City, Osaka, Japan

SPACING CHARTS

GRAINS

recommended spacing

Rye	—	3, 4, 5 & 6″
Wheat	—	3, 4, 5 & 6″
Soybeans	—	4, 6, 9 & 12″
Peanuts	—	6, 9 & 12″
Rice	—	3, 4, 5 & 6″
Beans, Pinto	—	6″
Kidney	—	6″

BERRIES AND GRAPES

Blackberries	—	4′	2′ wide beds
Boysenberries	—	8′	2′ wide beds
Currants	—	4′	2′ wide beds
Grapes	—	8′	2′ wide beds
Raspberries	—	4′	2′ wide beds
Strawberries	—	12″	2′ wide beds

COVER CROPS

Clovers	—⎱	2 oz. broadcast per 100 sq. ft.
Alfalfa	—⎰	(4 heaping tablespoons)
Cowpeas	—	3′
Fava Beans	—	8″

FIBER

Cotton —	12″
Flax —	3, 4″

recommended spacing

• Grains and cover crops are generally short germinating seeds (1-7 days).

FRUIT BUSHES AND TREES

Bush Fruit "Trees" — 3' centers, 3' high —Plum and sweet and sour cherries available

Dwarf Fruit Trees — 8' centers, 8' high —Apple, cherry, peach, nectarine, pear and apricot available

- See books under "Tree" heading and two Rodale entries under "General" heading in Bibliography for information on general care of these crops.

HERB SPACING CHART

Annuals—plant seed in spring for late summer harvest

	height	inches apart		height	inches apart
Anise	2'	8	Chervil	1½'	4
Sweet Basil	1–2'	12	Coriander	1–1½'	6
Borage	1½'	15	Dill	2½'	8
Caraway	2½'	6	Fennel	3–5'	12
Chamomile	2½'	6–10	Parsley	2½'	10
(*Matricaria chamomilla*)			Summer Savory	1½'	6

Perennials — need a permanent place in the garden

	height	inches apart			height	inches apart	
Angelica	4–6'	36		Santolina	2'	30	
*Bee Balm	3'	30		Winter Savory	1'	12	
Burnet	15"	15		Southernwood	3–5'	30	
Catnip	2–3'	15	(spreads)**	*Spearmint	2–3'	15	(spreads)**
*Chamomile, Roman	3–12"	12		Stinging Nettle	4–6'	24	(spreads)**
(*Anthemis nobilis*)				Tansy	4'	30	
Chives	10–24"	5		Tarragon	2'	18	
Costmary	2–6'	12		Thyme	1'	6	
Comfrey	15–36"	15–36		Valerian	4'	18	
*Feverfew	1–3'	10–15		*Woodruff	6–10"	8–12 (spreads)**	
Horehound	2'	9	(spreads)**	Wormwood	3–5'	12	
Hyssop	2'	12		Yarrow—Common	3–5'	12	
Lavender	3'	24		(*Achillea millefolium*)			
Lemon Balm	3'	12	(spreads)**	*Yarrow—White, red			
Lemon Verbena	10'	24		or pink flowered			
Lovage	6'	36		*Scented Geraniums			
Marjoram	1'	12		Rose	3'	30	
*Oregano	2'	18–24		Lemon	2–3'	***	
Peppermint	2½'	12	(spreads)**	Apple	10"	18	
*Pineapple Sage	4'	36		Peppermint	2'	48	
Rosemary	3'	36		Coconut	8–12"	18	
Rue	3'	18		Lime	***	***	
Sage	2'	18					

* Based on our experience. Others are from the *Herb Chart* by Evelyn Gregg, Biodynamic Farming and Gardening Assn., Wyoming, Rhode Island.

** Spreads underground—keep it contained or plant where it can keep going.
*** Do not yet know height and/or spacing information.

NOTE: Many herbs are long germinating seeds (22–28 days). Most perennials started from cuttings or root divisions; perennials started from seed take 1–4 years to reach full size.

FLOWER SPACING CHART

Spacings vary for flowers depending on the variety and how the flowers are used. The following may help you start out with the most common flowers.

Annuals — replant each year from seed

	height	inches apart*		height	inches apart*
African Daisy	4–16″	12	Phlox	6–18″	9
Aster	1–3′	10–12	(*P. Drummondii*)**		
Calif. Poppy***	9–12″	12	Portulaca	6″	6–9
Columbine	2–3′	12	Pansy	6–9″	8–10
Calendula***	1½–2′	12	Scabiosa	2½–3′	12–18
Cosmos***	2–3′	12–18	Scarlet Sage.	12–18″	12
Flowering Tobacco	3′	18–24	(*Salvia splendens*)		
Hollyhock***	4–6′	12	Schizanthus	1½–2′	12–18
Marigold, African	2–4′	12–24	Shirley Poppy	1½–2′	18
Marigold, French	6–18″	8–12	Snapdragons	1½–3′	12
Nasturtium, Dwarf***	12″	8	Stocks	12–30″	12
Nasturtium, Climbing***	Trails	10	Strawflower	2–3′	12–18
Petunia	12–16″	12	Sweet Peas	Climbing	12
			Zinnia	1–3′	12–18

Perennials — need a permanent space in the garden

	height	inches apart		height	inches apart
Alyssum	4–6″	10–12	Gazania	6–12″	10
(*Lobularia maritima*)			Iceland Poppy	1′	12
Aubrieta	Trailing	12–15	Jacob's Ladder	6″–3′	12–15
Baby's Breath	3–4′	14–16	(*Polemonium caeruleum*)		
Bachelor Buttons	2′	12	Marguerite	2½–3′	18–24
Carnation	1′	12	Oriental Poppy	2½–3′	12–14
Chrysanthemum	2–3′	18–24	Pinks (*Dianthus*)	1′	12
Coral Bells	2′	12′	Peony	2′	14–16
(*Heuchera sanguinea*)			Painted Daisy	3′	12
Coreopsis	2′	9–18	Scabiosa	2′	12
Delphinium	1–5′	24	Sea Pink (*Armeria*)	4–6″	10–12
Foxglove	3′	12	Shasta Daisy	2½–3′	12
Gaillardia	2–3′	12	Sweet William	1–2′	12

* These are spacings for standard-sized plants. For smaller varieties, the spacings should be reduced in proportion to the reduced plant size.

** Botanical Latin names also given when confusion might occur without it.

***Reseed themselves easily by dropping many seeds on ground.

NOTE: Most flowers are long germinating seeds (8–21 days).

Use this space to record your favorite flowers and herbs which are not included in the preceding spacing charts. *Use within-the-row spacings given on the back of the seed packets.*

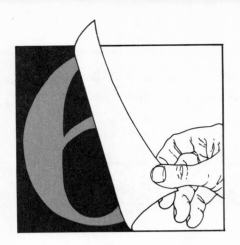

Making The Garden Plan

Now we come to the art of putting the theory into a garden plan. No book is detailed enough to make gardening foolproof. If growing plants didn't involve real learning and *experimentation* it would not be nearly so satisfying. The plans that follow are meant to illustrate some of the considerations that make a successful garden. They are based on what the average American consumes each year, but do not take the precise amounts too seriously. Everyone has different tastes and your use of the "Average American Diet" changes rapidly when you have fresh abundant vegetables to use.

Before you start, there is some local information you will need. Talk to neighbors who garden, check with the county agricultural agent, or ask at the local nursery. You want to know:

Which vegetables grow well in your area?

When does the main planting season start?

What is the soil like?

Are there any special climatic conditions to be aware of, such as heavy winds, hot dry spells or excessive rain? How do people usually plan for this?

The first plan is for a 1 person garden. The first year includes the easiest crops to grow in 100 square feet based on yields expected of a good gardener. The second year, the square footage doubles and more difficult crops are added. The third and fourth years, trees, herbs, strawberries and asparagus are included—these permanent plantings being placed in soil that has now been worked for two years. After 3 or 4 years, the skills gained may enable one to condense vegetable growing from 200 square feet to 100 square feet, leaving 100 square feet for fruit trees and strawberries and 100 square feet for grains (wheat, rye, lentils, soybeans), fibers (cotton or flax) or special interest crops (chicken, goat or bee forage, grapes, blueberries, bamboo, herbs, nut trees, and so on).

Lastly, a garden plan for a family of four is shown. We recommend using a similar 3-4 year progression, starting with approximately 300 square feet the first year.

Buying seeds for a backyard garden easily runs up a $10-20 bill. At our garden supply store in Palo Alto we purchase seeds in bulk and sell them out of jars like penny candy using teaspoons and tablespoons to measure. One can easily spend less than $2 in our store for 6 months of vegetables. You can take advantage of the same low prices by having bulk seeds ordered and carried at your local co-op grocery store.

The plans specify twice as many seedlings as are needed in the garden beds. Plant the best ones and give any extras to a friend. Leaf lettuce matures sooner than head lettuce. Planting both insures a continuous harvest. Similarly, half of the tomatoes planted should be an early variety (maturing in 65 days) for continuous harvesting. Save space by tying tomatoes up to stakes and training cucumbers on a trellis. Pumpkins take a lot of space. Plant them at the edge of the garden where they can sprawl over uncultivated areas. Corn is pollinated by the wind. A square block of 4 plants in each direction is the minimum for adequate pollination. In small plantings you may want to hand-pollinate it so all ears can fill out optimally.

THE GARDEN YEAR

Winter
☐ Plan Garden
☐ Order seeds (allow 2 months for delivery if ordering by mail)
☐ Make flats, trellises, mini-greenhouses, etc.

Spring
☐ Plant flats so they can mature while soil is being prepared
☐ Start new compost piles with plentiful weeds and grass clippings
☐ Spread fall compost and dig garden beds
☐ Plant throughout spring and early summer

Summer
☐ Plant summer crops
☐ Keep garden watered and weeded
☐ Harvest and enjoy the fruits of your work
☐ In mild winter areas, plant fall gardens at the end of summer.

Fall
☐ Start additional compost piles with plentiful leaves and garden waste
☐ Harvest summer crops.

ONE PERSON MINI-GARDEN, *FIRST* YEAR, 6 MONTH GROWING SEASON
100 SQUARE FEET

6 weeks before last frost of spring _____
(date)

Start seedlings in flats:
cabbage	— 8 seeds
broccoli	— 4 seeds
leaf lettuce	—10 seeds
head lettuce	— 6 seeds

2 weeks before last frost of spring _____
(date)

Set out:
cabbage	— 4 plants	6.7	sq. ft.
broccoli	— 2 plants	3.2	sq. ft.
leaf lettuce	— 5 plants	5.25	sq. ft.
head lettuce	— 3 plants		

Plant:
bush peas	—218 seeds	6.8	sq. ft.
carrots	— 96 seeds	3	sq. ft.
beets	— 17 seeds	1	sq. ft.
onions	— 60 sets	3.8	sq. ft.
radishes	— 43 seeds	.25	sq. ft.

Start seedlings in flats:
tomatoes	—8 seeds
peppers	—8 seeds
sweet basil	—2 seeds
zinnias	—6 seeds
cucumbers	—8 seeds

On last frost date _____
(date)

Plant:
potatoes	—35 starts (4.4 lbs.)	35 sq. ft.

2 weeks after last frost date _____
(date)

Set out:
tomatoes	—4 plants	15	sq. ft
bell peppers	—4 plants	4	sq. ft.
sweet basil	—1 plant	1	sq. ft.
cucumbers	—4 plants	4	sq. ft.
zinnias	—3 plants	3	sq. ft.

Plant:
pumpkins	—1 seed	6.3	sq. ft.
zucchini	—1 seed	2.3	sq. ft.

6-8 weeks after last frost _____
(date)

As first crops come out, plant:
early corn	—24 seeds	20	sq. ft.
bush limas	—36 seeds	9	sq. ft.
cosmos	— 1 seed	1	sq. ft.

14 weeks after last frost _____
(date)

As potatoes come out, plant:
corn	—32 seeds	25	sq. ft.
bush green beans	—25 seeds	10	sq. ft.

8–12 weeks before first frost _____
(date)

Start seedlings in flats:
leaf lettuce	— 16 seeds
head lettuce	— 10 seeds
broccoli	— 2 seeds
stocks	— 5 seeds
calendulas	— 5 seeds

4-8 weeks before first frost of fall _____
(date)

As early corn comes out, set out:
leaf lettuce	— 8 plants	7.8	sq. ft.
head lettuce	— 5 plants		
broccoli	— 1 plant	1.6	sq. ft.
stocks	— 5 plants	5	sq. ft.
calendulas	— 5 plants	5	sq. ft.

Plant:
carrots	— 96 seeds	2.7	sq. ft.
peas	— 218 seeds	6.8	sq. ft.
chard	— 2 seeds	1	sq. ft.
radishes	— 43 seeds	.25	sq. ft.

Spring
BED 1

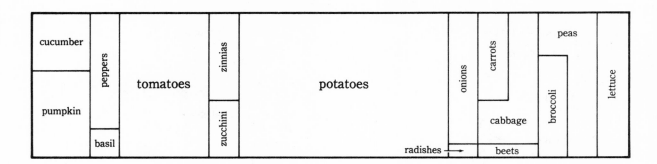

cucumber

peppers

tomatoes

zinnias

potatoes

onions

carrots

peas

lettuce

pumpkin

basil

zucchini

cabbage

broccoli

radishes → beets

Summer
(BED 1)

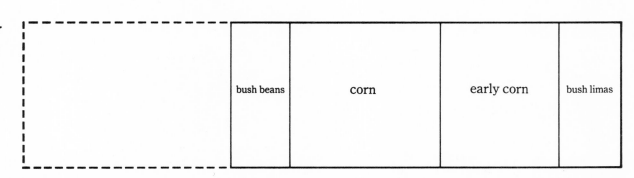

bush beans

corn

early corn

bush limas

Fall
(BED 1)

peas

lettuce

← radishes

stocks

carrots

broccoli chard

calendulas

Scale: 5/16 inch to 1 foot

6 weeks before last frost of spring _____
(date)

Start seedlings in flats:

cabbage	—	8 seeds
broccoli	—	4 seeds
brussels sprouts	—	2 seeds
cauliflower	—	2 seeds
leaf lettuce	—	16 seeds
head lettuce	—	10 seeds
celery	—	16 seeds
parsley	—	2 seeds

2 weeks before last frost _____
(date)

Set out:

cabbage	— 4 plants	5.2	sq. ft.
broccoli	— 2 plants	2.6	sq. ft.
cauliflower	— 1 plant	1.3	sq. ft.
brussels sprouts	— 1 plant	2.3	sq. ft.
leaf lettuce	— 8 plants	7.8	sq. ft.
head lettuce	— 5 plants		

Plant:

spinach	— 20 seeds	2.2	sq. ft.
peas	— 218 seeds	6.8	sq. ft.
carrots	— 96 seeds	2.7	sq. ft.
beets	— 17 seeds	1	sq. ft.
onion sets	— 60 sets	3.8	sq. ft.
radishes	— 43 seeds	.25	sq. ft.
garlic	— 5 cloves	.3	sq. ft.

Start seedling in flats:

tomatoes	—	10 seeds
bell peppers	—	8 seeds
eggplant	—	2 seeds
dill	—	2 seeds

On last frost date_____
(date)

Plant:
potatoes —86 starts (10.7 lbs.)   40.2 sq. ft.

Start seedlings in flats:

cucumbers	—	8 seeds
sweet basil	—	2 seeds
cantaloup	—	8 seeds
honeydew melons	—	8 seeds
watermelons	—	8 seeds
zinnias	—	3 seeds
cosmos	—	3 seeds

2 weeks after last frost _____
(date)

Set out:

tomatoes	— 5 plants	20	sq. ft.
eggplant	— 1 plant	2.3	sq. ft.
bell peppers	— 4 plants	4	sq. ft.
parsley	— 1 plant	.7	sq. ft.

Plant:

corn	— 32 seeds	25	sq. ft.

Move celery to deeper flat.

4 weeks after last frost _____
(date)

Set out:

cucumbers	— 4 plants	4	sq. ft.
sweet potatoes	— 8 starts (1.3 lbs.)	4.5	sq. ft.
dill	— 1 plant	.4	sq. ft.
sweet basil	— 1 plant	1	sq. ft.
cantaloup	— 4 plants	12.5	sq. ft.
honeydew melons	— 4 plants	16	sq. ft.
watermelons	— 4 plants	16	sq. ft.
zinnias	— 3 plants	3	sq. ft.
cosmos	— 3 plants	3	sq. ft.

Plant:

bush green beans	—36 seeds	14	sq. ft.
bush lima beans	—32 seeds	9	sq. ft.
pumpkins	— 1 seed	6.3	sq. ft.
zucchini	— 1 seed	2.3	sq. ft.

8 weeks after last frost _____
(date)

As first planting comes out, plant:
potatoes —86 starts (10.7 lbs.)   40.2 sq. ft.

12 weeks after frost _____
(date)

Start seedlings in flats:

broccoli	—	4 seeds
cabbage	—	8 seeds
stocks	—	10 seeds
leaf lettuce	—	16 seeds
head lettuce	—	10 seeds
calendulas	—	10 seeds

Set out:

celery	— 8 plants	2	sq. ft.

14 weeks after frost _____
(date)

As first potatoes come out, plant:

corn	—32 seeds	25	sq. ft.

(early variety: 60-65 day maturation)

16 weeks after frost_____
(date)

Set out:

broccoli	— 1 plant	1.3	sq. ft.
leaf lettuce	— 8 plants	7.8	sq. ft.
head lettuce	— 5 plants	2.7	sq. ft.
calendulas	— 4 plants	4	sq. ft.
stocks	— 4 plants	4	sq. ft.
cabbage	— 4 plants	5.2	sq. ft.

Plant:

chard	— 2 seeds	1	sq. ft.
radishes	— 43 seeds	.25	sq. ft.
peas	— 218 seeds	6.8	sq. ft.
carrots	— 96 seeds	2.7	sq. ft.
spinach	— 20 seeds	2.2	sq. ft.

NOTE: By the second year, the curved bed surface gives you 120 square feet of planting area in each 100 square feet of bed.

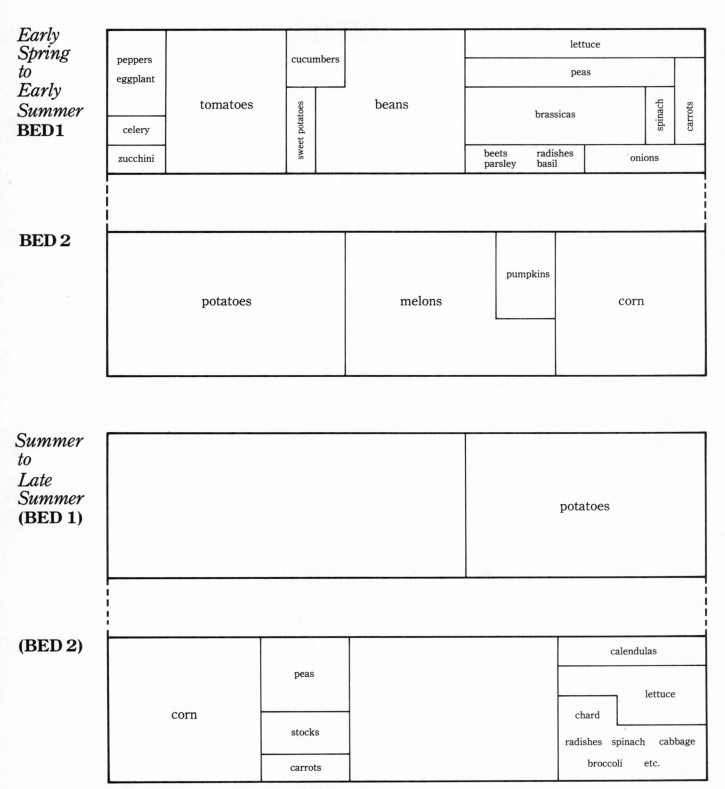

Early Spring to Early Summer **BED 1**

peppers eggplant	tomatoes	cucumbers	beans	lettuce
celery		sweet potatoes		peas
zucchini				brassicas / spinach / carrots
				beets parsley / radishes basil / onions

BED 2

potatoes   melons   pumpkins   corn

Summer to Late Summer **(BED 1)**

potatoes

(BED 2)

corn   peas   stocks   carrots   calendulas   lettuce   chard   radishes spinach cabbage   broccoli etc.

Scale: 5/16 inch to 1 foot

ONE PERSON MINI-GARDEN, *THIRD* YEAR, 6 MONTH GROWING SEASON
380 SQUARE FEET (including paths)

As early as possible in spring plant:

1 bare root fruit tree	—64 sq. ft.	
8 asparagus roots	— 8 sq. ft.	
20 strawberries	— 20 sq. ft.	

6 weeks before last frost of spring _____
(date)

Start seedlings in flats:

cabbage	— 8 seeds
broccoli	— 4 seeds
brussels sprouts	— 2 seeds
cauliflower	— 2 seeds
leaf lettuce	—16 seeds
head lettuce	—10 seeds
celery	—16 seeds
parsley	— 2 seeds

2 weeks before last frost _____
(date)

Start seedlings in flats:

tomatoes	—10 seeds
bell peppers	— 8 seeds
eggplant	— 2 seeds
dill	— 2 seeds

Set out:

cabbage	—4 plants	5.2	sq. ft.
broccoli	—2 plants	2.6	sq. ft.
cauliflower	—1 plant	1.3	sq. ft.
brussels sprouts	—1 plant	2.3	sq. ft.
leaf lettuce	—8 plants	7.8	sq. ft.
head lettuce	—5 plants		

Plant:

spinach	— 20 seeds	2.2	sq. ft.
peas	—218 seeds	6.8	sq. ft.
carrots	— 96 seeds	2.7	sq. ft.
beets	— 17 seeds	1	sq. ft.
onions	— 60 sets	3.8	sq. ft.
radishes	— 43 seeds	.25	sq. ft.
garlic	— 5 cloves	.3	sq. ft.

On last frost date_____
(date)

Plant:

potatoes	107 starts (13.4 lbs.)	50	sq. ft.

Start seedlings in flats:

cucumbers	— 8 seeds
sweet basil	— 2 seeds
cantaloup	— 8 seeds
honeydew melons	— 8 seeds
watermelons	— 8 seeds
dill	— 2 seeds
zinnias	—10 seeds
cosmos	—10 seeds

2 weeks after last frost _____
(date)

Set out:

tomatoes	—5 plants	20	sq. ft.
eggplant	—1 plant	2.3	sq. ft.
bell peppers	—4 plants	4	sq. ft.
parsley	—1 plant	.7	sq. ft.

Plant:

corn	—64 seeds	50	sq. ft.

Move celery to deeper flat

4 weeks after last frost _____
(date)

Set out:

cucumbers	— 4 plants	4	sq. ft.
sweet potatoes	— 8 starts	4.5	sq. ft.
	(1.3 lbs.)		
dill	— 1 plant	.4	sq. ft.
sweet basil	— 1 plant	1	sq. ft.
cantaloup	— 4 plants	12.5	sq. ft.
honeydew melons	— 4 plants		
watermelons	— 4 plants	16	sq. ft.
zinnias	— 5 plants	5	sq. ft.
cosmos	— 5 plants	5	sq. ft.
celery	— 8 plants	2	sq. ft.

Plant:

bush green beans	—36 seeds	14	sq. ft.
bush lima beans	—32 seeds	9	sq. ft.
pumpkins	— 1 seed	6.3	sq. ft.
zucchini	— 1 seed	2.3	sq. ft.

8 weeks after last frost _____
(date)

As first planting comes out plant:

potatoes	—64 starts	30	sq. ft.
	(8 lbs.)		

12 weeks after frost _____
(date)

Start seedlings in flats:

broccoli	— 4 seeds
cabbage	— 8 seeds
stocks	—10 seeds
leaf lettuce	—16 seeds
head lettuce	—10 seeds
calendulas	—10 seeds

16 weeks after frost _____
(date)

Set out:

cabbage	—4 plants	5.2	sq. ft.

				Plant:			
stocks	—4 plants	4	sq. ft.	chard	—	2 seeds	1 sq. ft.
calendula	—4 plants	4	sq. ft.	carrots	—	96 seeds	2.7 sq. ft.
broccoli	—1 plant	1.3	sq. ft.	radishes	—	43 seeds	.25 sq. ft.
leaf lettuce	—8 plants		7.8 sq. ft.	peas	—	218 seeds	6.8 sq. ft.
head lettuce	—5 plants						

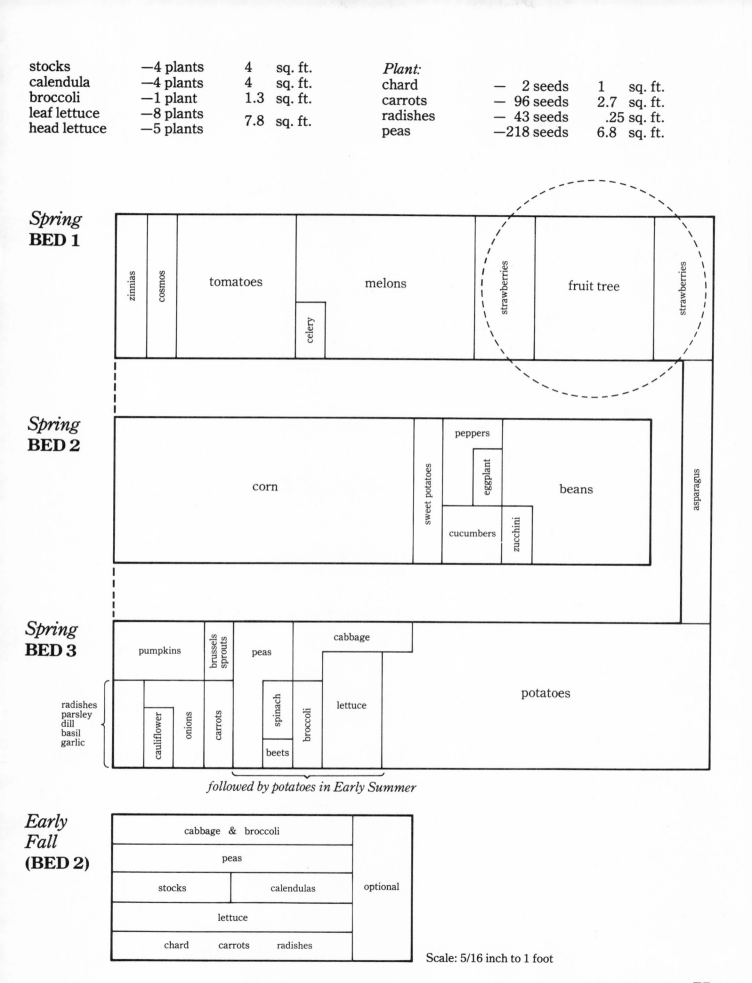

Spring
BED 1

zinnias · cosmos · tomatoes · celery · melons · strawberries · fruit tree · strawberries

Spring
BED 2

corn · sweet potatoes · peppers · eggplant · cucumbers · zucchini · beans · asparagus

Spring
BED 3

pumpkins · brussels sprouts · peas · cabbage · cauliflower · onions · carrots · spinach · beets · broccoli · lettuce · potatoes

radishes
parsley
dill
basil
garlic

followed by potatoes in Early Summer

Early
Fall
(BED 2)

cabbage & broccoli · peas · stocks · calendulas · lettuce · chard · carrots · radishes · optional

Scale: 5/16 inch to 1 foot

As soon as possible in spring, plant:

dwarf fruit tree	— 1 tree	64	sq. ft.
strawberries	—20 plants	20	sq. ft.
lavender	— 1 plant	4	sq. ft.
sage	— 1 plant	2.3	sq. ft.
marjoram	— 1 plant	1	sq. ft.
chives	— 3 plants	.5	sq. ft.

OR whatever herbs desired

6 weeks before last frost of spring _____
(date)

Start seedlings in flats:

cabbage	— 8 seeds
broccoli	— 4 seeds
brussels sprouts	— 2 seeds
cauliflower	— 2 seeds
leaf lettuce	—16 seeds
head lettuce	—10 seeds
celery	—16 seeds
parsley	— 2 seeds
dill	— 2 seeds

2 weeks before last frost _____
(date)

Set out:

cabbage	—4 plants	5.2	sq. ft.
broccoli	—2 plants	2.6	sq. ft.
cauliflower	—1 plant	1.3	sq. ft.
brussels sprouts	—1 plant	2.3	sq. ft.
leaf lettuce	—8 plants	7.8	sq. ft.
head lettuce	—5 plants		

Plant:

peas	—218 seeds	6.8	sq. ft.
carrots	— 96 seeds	2.7	sq. ft.
beets	— 17 seeds	1	sq. ft.
onions	— 60 sets	3.8	sq. ft.
radishes	— 43 seeds	.25	sq. ft.
garlic	— 5 sets	.3	sq. ft.

Start seedlings in flats:

tomatoes	—10 seeds
bell peppers	— 8 seeds
eggplant	— 2 seeds

On last frost date _____
(date)

Plant:

potatoes	87 starts (10.7 lbs)	40	sq. ft.

Start seedlings in flats:

cucumbers	—8 seeds
sweet basil	—4 seeds
cantaloup	—8 seeds
watermelons	—8 seeds

2 weeks after last frost _____
(date)

Set out:

tomatoes	— 5 plants	20	sq. ft.
eggplant	— 1 plant	2.3	sq. ft.
bell peppers	— 4 plants	4	sq. ft.
parsley	— 1 plant	.7	sq. ft.

Plant:

corn	—32 seeds	25	sq. ft.

Move celery to deeper flat:

4 weeks after last frost _____
(date)

Set out:

cucumbers	—4 plants	4	sq. ft.
sweet potatoes	—8 starts (1.3 lbs.)	4.5	sq. ft.
dill	—1 plant	.4	sq. ft.
sweet basil	—1 plant	1	sq. ft.
cantaloup	—4 plants	12.5	sq. ft.
honeydew melons	—4 plants		
watermelons	—4 plants	16	sq. ft.
celery	—8 plants	2	sq. ft.

Plant:

bush green beans	—36 seeds	14	sq. ft.
bush lima beans	—32 seeds	9	sq. ft.
pumpkins	— 1 seed	6.3	sq. ft.

8 weeks after last frost _____
(date)

As first planting comes out plant:
potatoes —87 starts (10.7 lbs.) 40 sq. ft.

12 weeks after frost _____
(date)

Start seedlings in flats:

broccoli	— 4 seeds
cabbage	— 8 seeds
stocks	—10 seeds
leaf lettuce	—16 seeds
head lettuce	—10 seeds
calendulas	—10 seeds

14 weeks after frost _____
(date)

As first potatoes come out plant:
corn —32 seeds 25 sq. ft.
(early variety 60-65 days maturation)

16 weeks after frost _____
(date)

Set out:

broccoli	— 1 plant	1.6	sq. ft.
leaf lettuce	— 8 plants	7.8	sq. ft.
head lettuce	— 5 plants		
cabbage	— 4 plants	5.2	sq. ft.
stocks	— 5 plants	5	sq. ft.
calendulas	— 5 plants	5	sq. ft.

Plant:

carrots	— 96 seeds	2.7	sq. ft.
chard	— 2 seeds	1	sq. ft.
radishes	— 43 seeds	.24	sq. ft.
peas	—218 seeds	6.8	sq. ft.
spinach	— 20 seeds	2.2	sq. ft.

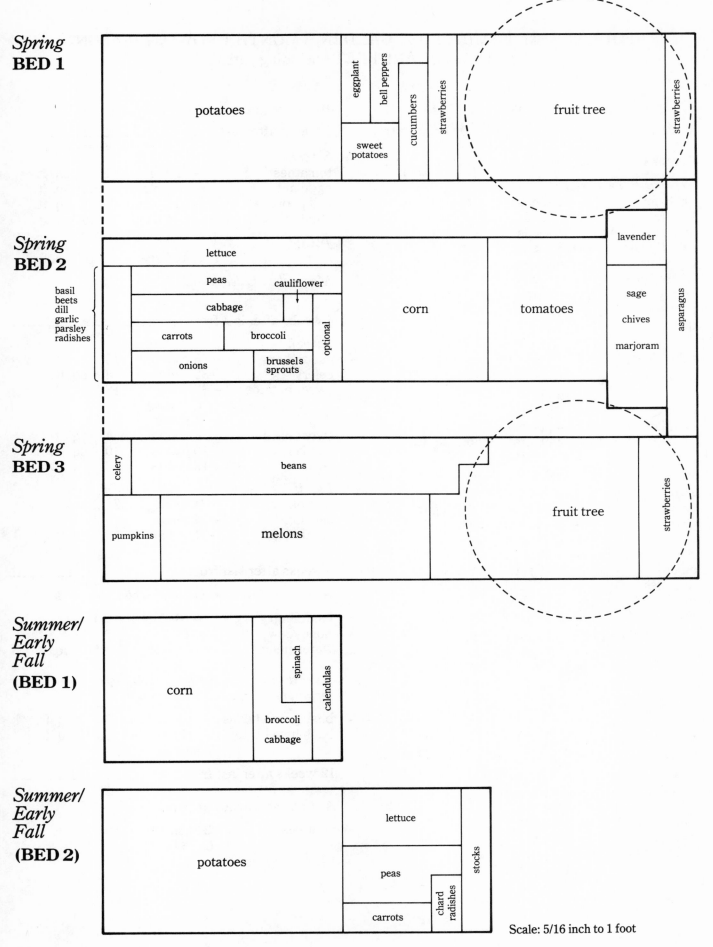

Spring **BED 1**

potatoes

eggplant

bell peppers

sweet potatoes

cucumbers

strawberries

fruit tree

strawberries

Spring **BED 2**

basil
beets
dill
garlic
parsley
radishes

lettuce

peas

cauliflower

cabbage

carrots

broccoli

onions

brussels sprouts

optional

corn

tomatoes

lavender

sage

chives

marjoram

asparagus

Spring **BED 3**

celery

beans

pumpkins

melons

fruit tree

strawberries

Summer/ Early Fall **(BED 1)**

corn

spinach

broccoli

cabbage

calendulas

Summer/ Early Fall **(BED 2)**

potatoes

lettuce

peas

carrots

chard

radishes

stocks

Scale: 5/16 inch to 1 foot

FOUR PERSON FAMILY FOOD GARDEN, 6 MONTH GROWING SEASON
1,302 SQUARE FEET (including paths)

As soon as possible in spring, plant: 7 dwarf fruit trees

6 weeks before last frost of spring _____
(date)

Start seedlings in flats:

cabbage	—32 seeds
broccoli	—16 seeds
brussels sprouts	— 8 seeds
cauliflower	— 8 seeds
head lettuce	—64 seeds
leaf lettuce	—40 seeds
celery	—64 seeds
parsley	— 8 seeds
dill	— 8 seeds

2 weeks before last frost _____
(date)

Set out:

cabbage	—16 plants		
broccoli	— 8 plants		
cauliflower	— 4 plants		
brussels sprouts	— 4 plants	55.2	sq. ft.
leaf lettuce	—32 plants		
head lettuce	—20 plants	31.2	sq. ft.

Plant:

spinach	— 80 seeds	8.8	sq. ft.
peas	—1,744 seeds	54.4	sq. ft.
carrots	— 768 seeds	24	sq. ft.
beets	— 68 seeds	4	sq. ft.
onions	— 240 sets	15.2	sq. ft.
radishes	— 172 seeds	1	sq. ft.
garlic	— 20 cloves	1.2	sq. ft.
chard	— 11 seeds	4	sq. ft.

Start seedlings in flats:

tomatoes	—40 seeds
bell peppers	—32 seeds
eggplant	— 8 seeds

On last frost date _____
(date)

Plant:

potatoes	— 471 starts (59 lbs.)	220	sq. ft.

Start Flats:

cantaloup	—32 seeds
honeydew	—32 seeds
watermelons	—32 seeds
cucumbers	—32 seeds
sweet basil	— 8 seeds
zinnias	—20 seeds
cosmos	—20 seeds

2 weeks after last frost _____
(date)

Set out:

tomatoes	— 20 plants	80	sq. ft.
eggplant	— 4 plants	9.2	sq. ft.
bell peppers	— 16 plants	16	sq. ft.
parsley	— 4 plants	2.8	sq. ft.

Plant:

corn	— 128 seeds	100	sq. ft.

Move celery to deeper flat

4 weeks after last frost _____
(date)

Set out:

cucumbers	—16 plants	16	sq. ft.
celery	—32 plants	8	sq. ft.
sweet potatoes	—32 starts (5.2 lbs.)	18	sq. ft.
dill	— 4 plants	1.6	sq. ft.
sweet basil	— 4 plants	4	sq. ft.
zinnias	—10 plants	10	sq. ft.
cosmos	—12 plants	12	sq. ft.

Plant:

pumpkins	— 4 seeds	25.2	sq. ft.
zucchini	— 4 seeds	9.2	sq. ft.
sunflowers	— 4 seeds	15	sq. ft.

6 weeks after last frost _____
(date)

As peas and carrots come out, replant bed with:

canteloup	—16 plants	50	sq. ft.
honeydew	—16 plants	50	sq. ft.
watermelons	—16 plants	64	sq. ft.

As early brassicas and lettuce come out,
replant bed with:

bush green beans	—144 seeds	56	sq. ft.
bush lima beans	—128 seeds	36	sq. ft.

12 weeks after last frost _____
(date)

As first corn comes out, plant:

potatoes	—214 starts (26.8 lbs.)	100	sq. ft.

14 weeks after frost _____

(12 weeks before first frost of fall)   (date)

As first potatoes come out plant:

corn   —128 seeds   100 sq. ft.
(early variety: 60-65 day maturation)

Start flats:

broccoli   — 16 seeds
cabbage   — 32 seeds
stocks   — 20 seeds
leaf lettuce   — 64 seeds
head lettuce   — 40 seeds
calendulas   — 20 seeds

8 weeks before first fall frost_____

(date)

As last potatoes come out plant:

Set out:

broccoli   —   4 plants   6.4   sq. ft.
leaf lettuce   —   32 plants
head lettuce   —   20 plants   31.2 sq. ft.
calendulas   —   10 plants   10   sq. ft.
stocks   —   10 plants   10   sq. ft.
cabbage   —   16 plants   20.8 sq. ft.

Plant:

chard   —   8 seeds   4   sq. ft.
radishes   —172 seeds   1   sq. ft.
spinach   —   88 seeds   8   sq. ft.

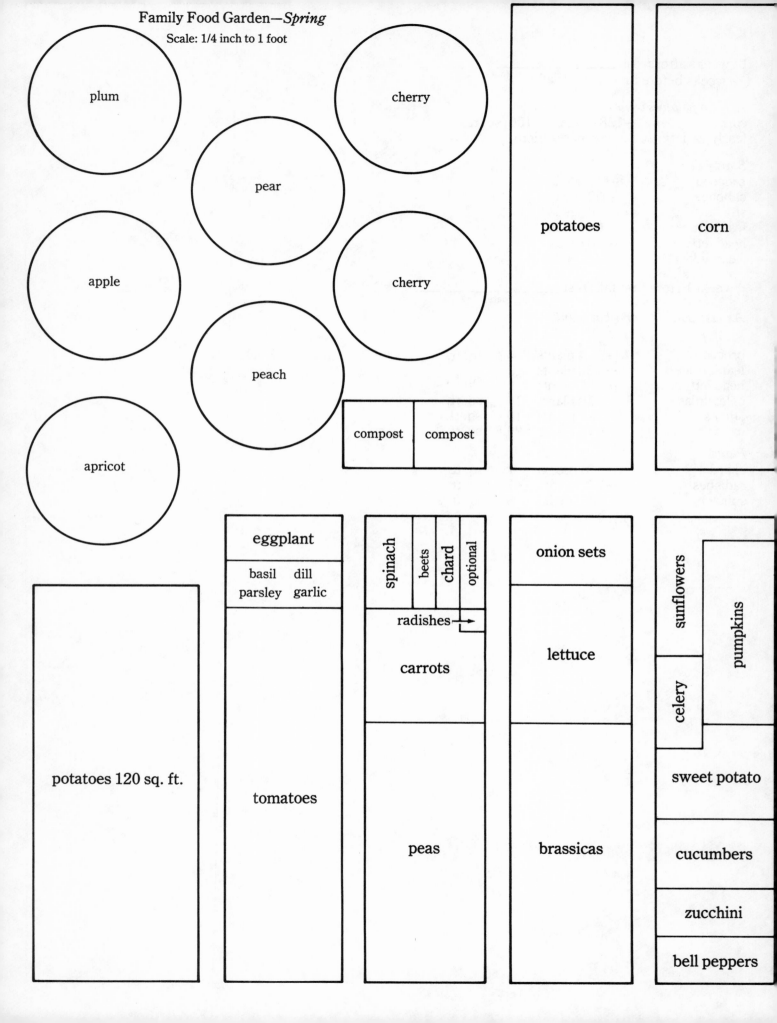

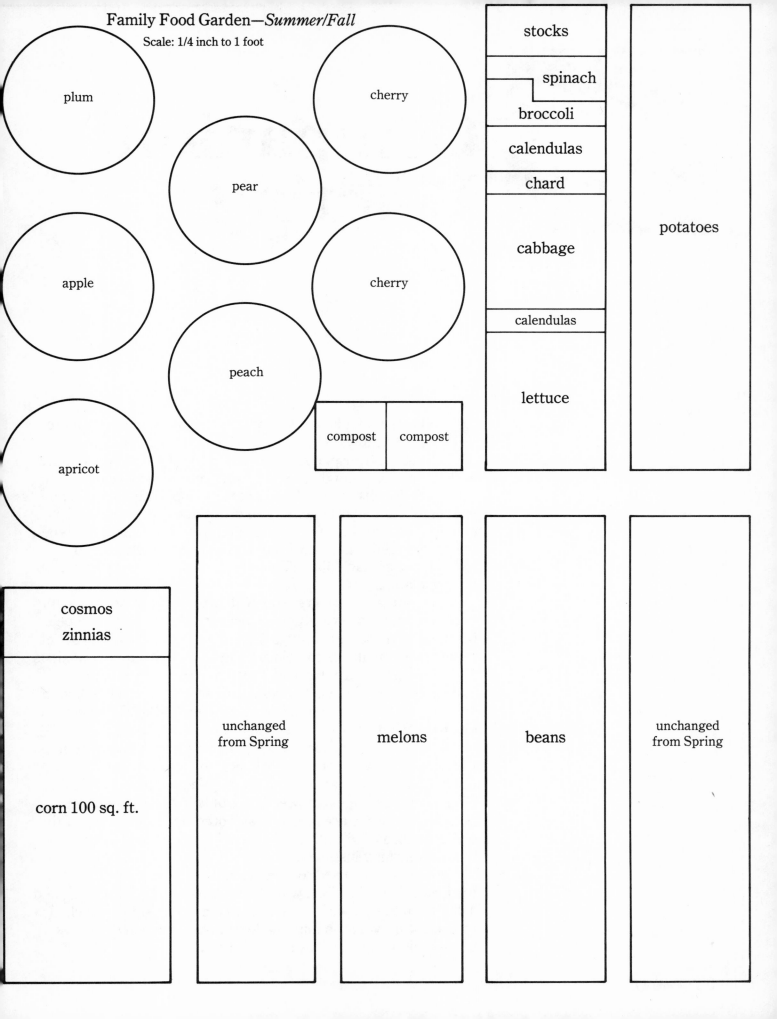

Family Food Garden—*Summer/Fall*

Scale: 1/4 inch to 1 foot

plum

cherry

pear

apple

cherry

peach

apricot

compost compost

stocks

spinach

broccoli

calendulas

chard

cabbage

calendulas

lettuce

potatoes

cosmos

zinnias

corn 100 sq. ft.

unchanged from Spring

melons

beans

unchanged from Spring

Companion Planting

Like people, plants like and dislike other members of the plant family, depending on the natures involved. Seedlings of transplanting size begin to relate more and more with the plants around them. These relationships become especially important as adult plants develop distinct personalities, essences and aromas. Green beans and strawberries, for example, thrive better when they are grown together than when they are grown separately. To get really good tasting bibb lettuce, one spinach plant should be grown with every four bibb lettuce plants.

In contrast, no plants grow well near wormwood due to its toxic leaf and root excretions. However, wormwood tea repels black fleas, discourages slugs, keeps beetles and weevils out of grain and combats aphids. So wormwood is not a totally noxious herb. Few plants are. Instead, they have their place in the natural order of things. Tomatoes are narcissistic. They like to be grown in compost made from their own bodies. They also like to be grown in the same area for a five year period.

Weeds are often specialists and doctors in the plant community. They take very well to a sick soil which needs to be built up and even seem to seek it out. Where cultivated garden plants could not manage, weeds are able to draw phosphorus, potash, calcium, trace minerals and other nutriments out of the soil and subsoil and concentrate them in their bodies. Plants seem to have uncanny instincts.

Weeds can be used to concentrate nutriments for future fertilization or to withdraw noxious elements, such as unwanted salts, from the growing area. A deficient soil is often enriched by the use of weeds in man-made compost or when their dead bodies are returned to the soil in nature.

Companion planting is the constructive use of plant relationships by the gardener, horticulturist and farmer. A scientific definition of companion planting is the placing together of plants having complementary physical demands. A more accurate, living and spiritual description is the growing together of all those elements and beings which encourage *life* and *growth*: the creation of a microcosm that includes vegetables, fruits, trees, bushes, wheat, flowers, weeds, birds, soil, microorganisms, water, nutriments, insects, toads, spiders and chickens.

Companion planting is still a new and very experimental field in which much more research needs to be performed. The age of the plants involved and the percentage of each of the types of plants grown together can be critical, as can be their relative proximity to one another. Companion planting should, therefore, be used with some caution and much observation. You may want to study the causes of some of these beneficial relationships. Are they due to root excretions, plant aroma or the pollen of composite flowers that attract certain beneficial predatory insects? Companion planting is a fascinating field.

Some of the companion planting techniques you can eventually try and experience are ones for Health; Nutrition; Physical Complementarity; and Weed, Insect and Animal Relationships.

Health

Better Growth—The growing together of green beans and strawberries and bibb lettuce and spinach has already been mentioned. On the other side of the spectrum, onions seriously inhibit the growth of beans and peas. In between the extremes, *bush* beans and beets may be grown together with no particular advantage or disadvantage to either plant. *Pole* beans and beets, on the other hand, do not get along well. The nuances are amazing. What is the difference between bush and pole beans? No one appears to know the scientific reason yet, but the difference can be observed. Ehrenreid Pheiffer developed a method known as crystallization from which one can predict in advance whether or not plants are good companions. In this technique, part of a plant is ground up and mixed with a chemical solution. After the solution dries, a crystalline pattern remains. Different plants have distinct, representative patterns. When two plant solutions are mixed, the patterns increase, decrease or stay the same in strength and regularity. Sometimes, both patterns improve, indicating a reciprocal, beneficial influence. Or both may deteriorate in a reciprocal negative reaction. One pattern may improve while another deteriorates, indicating a one-sided advantage. Both patterns may remain the same, indicating no particular companion advantage or disadvantage. And one plant pattern may increase or decrease in quality while the other undergoes no change. Two plants, which suffer a decrease in quality on a one-to-one basis, may show an increase in strength in a one-to-ten ratio.

Spacing for Better Companions—Using French intensive spacing with the plant leaves barely touching allows good companions to be better friends.

All Round Beneficial Influence—Certain herbs and one tree have a beneficial influence on the plant community. These plants and their characteristics are:[55]

☐ Lemon Balm
   Creates a beneficent atmosphere around itself and attracts bees. Part of the mint family.

☐ Marjoram
   Has a "beneficial effect on surrounding plants".

☐ Oregano
   Has a "beneficial effect on surrounding plants".

☐ Stinging Nettle (*Urtica dioica*)
   "Helps neighboring plants to grow more resistant to spoiling". Increases essential oil content in many herbs. "Stimulates humus formation." Helps stimulate fermentation in compost piles. As a tea, promotes plant growth and helps strengthen plants. Concentrates sulfur, potassium, calcium and iron in its body.

☐ Valerian (*Valeriana officinalis*)
   "Helps most vegetables". Stimulates phosphorus activity in its vicinity. Encourages health and disease resistance in plants.

☐ Chamomile (*Chamomile officinalis*)
   A lime specialist. "Contains a growth hormone which . . . stimulates the growth of yeast". In a 1:100 ratio helps growth of wheat. As a tea, combats diseases in young plants such as damping off. Concentrates calcium, sulfur and potash in its body.

☐ Dandelion (*Taraxacum officinale*)
   Increases "aromatic quality of all herbs." "In small amounts" helps most vegetables. Concentrates potash in its body.

☐ Oak Bark
   Concentrates calcium in its bark (bark is 77% calcium). In a special tea, it helps plants resist harmful diseases. The oak tree provides a beneficial influence around it which allows excellent soil to be produced underneath its branches. An excellent place to build a compost pile for the same reason, but keep the pile at least 6 feet from the tree trunk so an environment will not be created near the tree which is conducive to disease or attractive to harmful insects.

Note: Lemon blam, marjoram, oregano, and valerian are perennials. They are traditionally planted in a section along one end of the bed so they need not be disturbed when the bed is replanted.

Stinging nettle and tomatoes. Good garden companions.

55. Helen Philbrick and Richard B. Gregg, *Companion Plants and How To Use Them*, The Devin-Adair Company, Old Greenwich, Connecticut, 1966, pp. 16, 57, 58, 60, 65, 84, 85, 86, 92, 98.

Rudolf Steiner, *Agriculture—A Course of Eight Lectures*, Biodynamic Agricultural Association, London, 1958, pp. 93, 94, 95, 97, 99, 100.

Soil Life Stimulation—Stinging Nettle helps stimulate the microbiotic life in the soil and this helps plant growth.

Soil Improvement—Sow Thistle (*Sonchus oleraceus*) brings up nutriments from the subsoil to enrich a depleted topsoil. After years of dead Sow Thistle bodies have enriched the topsoil, heavier feeding grasses return. This is part of nature's recycling program in which leached out nutriments are returned to the topsoil as well as a natural method for raising new nutriment to the upper layers of the soil. It has been estimated that *one* rye plant grown in good soil produces an average of 3 miles of roots per day, 387 miles of roots during a season and 6,603 miles of root hairs. Plants are continuously providing their own composting program underground. In one year 800-1500 pounds of roots per acre are put into the soil by plants in a small garden, and red clover puts 1200-3850 pounds of roots into the soil in the same period of time.[56]

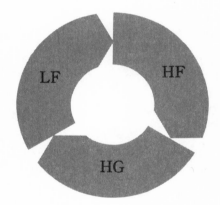

Plant root systems improve the topsoil by bringing up nutriments from the subsoil.

Nutrition

Over Time—Companion planting "over time" has been known for years as "crop rotation". After proper preparation of the soil, heavy feeders are planted. These are followed by heavy givers and then light feeders. This is a kind of *agricultural recycling* in which man and plants participate to return as much to the soil as has been taken out.

Heavy feeders, most of the vegetables we like and eat, (including corn, tomatoes, squash, lettuce, and cabbage) take a large amount of nutriment, especially nitrogen, from the soil. In the biodynamic/French intensive method, after heavy feeders have been harvested, phosphorous and potash are returned to the soil in the form of bone meal (phosphorous), wood ash (potash), and compost (usually phosphorous, potash and a little nitrogen). To return nitrogen to the soil, heavy givers are grown. Heavy givers are nitrogen-fixing plants or legumes: such as peas, beans, alfalfa, clover and vetch. Fava beans are good for this purpose. Not only do they bring large amounts of nitrogen into the soil, they also excrete substances which help eradicate tomato wilt causing organisims. (*Caution:* some people of Mediterranean descent *are fatally allergic* to fava beans even though they are very popular among these people. People on one tranquilizer have experienced the same reaction. Eat only one or two the first time.) After heavy givers, light feeders (all root crops) should be planted to give the soil a rest before the next heavy feeder onslaught. Three vegetables are low nitrogen lovers: turnips (a light feeder), sweet potatoes (a light feeder) and green peppers (a heavy feeder). The two light feeders would normally be planted after heavy givers, which put a lot of nitrogen into the soil. You may find it useful to have them follow a heavy feeder instead. It would also be good to have the green

LF   HF

HG

AGRICULTURAL RECYCLING

56. Helen Philbrick and Richard B. Gregg, *Companion Plants and How To Use Them*, The Devin-Adair Company, Old Greenwich, Connecticut, 1966, pp. 75-76.

pepper follow a heavy feeder. (It normally comes after a heavy giver and a light feeder.) You should experiment with these out of sequence plantings.

In Space—Companion planting of heavy feeders, heavy givers and light feeders can be done in the same growing area at the same time. For example, corn, beans and beets can be intermingled in the same bed. Just as with companion planting "over time", the gardener should proceed with care. In the above combination, the beans must be *bush* beans, since *pole* beans and beets do not grow well together. Also, pole beans have been reported to pull ears off the corn stalks. Pole beans have been grown successfully with corn, however; and a vegetable such as carrots may be substituted for the beets to allow you to use the tall beans. When different plants are grown together, you sacrifice some of the *living mulch* advantage to companion planting "in space" because of the different plant heights. One way to determine the spacing for different plants grown together, is to add their spacing together and divide by two. If you grow corn and beets together, add 15 inches to 3 inches for a total of 18 inches. Divided by 2, you get a per plant spacing of 9 inches. The beets, then, would be 9 inches from each corn plant and vice versa. Each corn plant will be 18 inches from each corn plant and each beet plant will be 18 inches from each beet plant. In the drawing below, note that each corn plant gets the 7-1/2 inches in each direction that it requires for a total of a growing area with a "diameter" of 15 inches. Each beet plant, at the same time, gets the 1-1/2 inches it requires in each direction for a growing space with a 3 inch "diameter". (See diagram below.)

TWO CROP COMPANION PLANTING
Circles show average root growth diameters

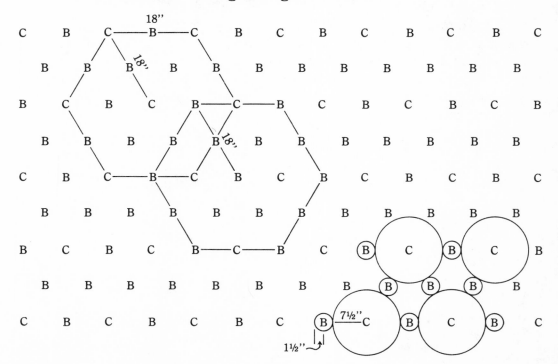

An easier, and probably just as effective method of companion planting "in space" is to divide your planting bed into separate sections (or beds within a bed) for each vegetable. In this method, a grouping of corn plants would be next to a group of bush beans and a group of beets. In reality, this is a kind of companion plant "over time" since there are heavy feeder, heavy giver and light feeder sections within a bed. Plant roots extend 1 to 4 feet around themselves, so it is also companion planting "in space". We recommend you use *this* approach. Additional spacing patterns no doubt exist and will be developed for companion planting "in space".

MULTI-CROP COMPANION PLANTING "IN SPACE"

corn	bush beans	beets	corn	bush beans	beets

A spacing example for 3 crops grown together—corn (a heavy feeder), bush beans (a heavy giver) and beets (a light feeder)—is given below. You should note that this approach to companion planting in space uses more bush bean and beet plants than corn and also contains some gaps in which still more bush beans and beets can be planted.

THREE CROP COMPANION PLANTING
Circles show average root growth diameters

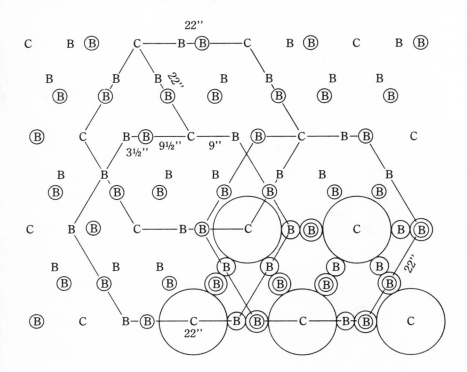

Compromise and Planning—You can see by now that companion planting involves selecting the combination of factors which works best in your soil and climate. Fortunately, the myriad of details fall into a pattern of simple guidelines. Within the guidelines, however, there are so many possible combinations that the planning process can become quite complex. Be easy on yourself. Only do as much companion planting as is easy for you and comes naturally. What you learn this year and become comfortable with, can be applied next year and so on. An easy place to start is with salad vegetables since these are generally companions. In contrast, onions, garlic, chives, and shallots have a harmful influence on peas and beans. Also, it is easier to companion plant over time rather than in space. Since you probably will not have enough area to use an entire bed for each crop, you might create several heavy feeder, heavy giver and light feeder sections within each bed. You may want to grow a preponderance of crops from one group such as the heavy feeders. (It is unlikely that you will want to grow 1/3 of each crop type.) Therefore, you will need to make adjustments, such as adding extra fertilizer and compost, when you follow one heavy feeder with another. Due to lack of space, you may have to grow a lot of plants together that are not companions. If so, you may need to be satisfied with lower yields, poorer quality vegetables and less healthy plants. Or, you might try to alter your diet to one which is still balanced but more in line with the balances of nature. At any rate, you can see it is useful to plan your garden in advance. You will need to know how many pounds of each vegetables you want during the year, how many plants are needed to grow the weight of vegetables you require, when to plant seeds both in flats and in the ground, when and how to rotate your crops and when to raise and transplant herbs so they will be at the peak of their own special influence. Use the charts at the end of the Seed Propagation section to assist in this work. To have their optimum effect as companions, herb plants should be reasonably mature when transplanted into a bed for insect control or general beneficial influence. It is easiest to plan your garden 12 months at a time and always at least 3 months in advance.

Physical Complementarity

Sun/Shade—Many plants have a special need for sunlight or a lack of it. Cucumbers, for example, are very hard to please. They like heat, moisture, a well-drained soil and some shade. One way to provide these conditions is to grow cucumbers with corn. The corn plants, which like heat and sun, can provide partial shade for the cucumber plants. Lettuce plants nestled among other plants for partial shade is another example. Sunflowers, which are tall and like lots of sun, should be planted at the north side of the garden. There they will not shade other plants and will receive enough sun for themselves.

Using the sun/shade technique is one way to make the most of your plants' physically complementary characteristics.

Lettuce plants can be nestled among other larger plants for partial shade.

Corn can provide the shade which cucumbers enjoy.

Shallow/Deep Rooting—There is no good, detailed example available. A dynamic process does occur over time, however, as plants with root systems of differing depths and breadths work different areas of the soil in the planting bed.[57]

Fast/Slow Maturing—The French intensive gardeners were able to grow as many as four crops in a growing bed at one time due to the staggered growth and maturation rates of different vegetables. The fact that the edible portions of the plants appear in different vertical locations also helped. Radishes, carrots, lettuce and cauliflower were grown together in one combination used by the French to take advantage of these differences.

Vertical Location of the Plant's Edible Portion—See Fast/Slow Maturing example.

Weed, Insect and Animal Relationships

"Weed" Control—Beets and members of the cabbage family are slowed down significantly by the presence of "weeds". To minimize the "weed" problem for sensitive plants, you can grow other plants during the previous season that discourage "weed" growth in the soil. Two such plants are kale and rape. Another example is the *Tagetes minuta*, a Mexican Marigold.[58] "In many instances it has killed even couch grass, convolvulus (wild morning glory), ground ivy, ground elder, horsetail and other persistent weeds that defy most poisons. Its lethal action works only on starch roots and had no effect on woody ones like roses, fruit bushes and shrubs. Where it had grown, the soil was enriched as well as cleansed, its texture was refined and lumps of clay were broken up."[59] Some care should be taken when using this marigold, however, since vegetable crops may also be killed by it and the plant does give off toxic excretions. Tests should be performed to determine how long the influence of these excretions stay with the soil. But to cleanse a soil of pernicious weeds and thereby get it ready for vegetables, *Tagetes minuta* appears to be a useful plant.

Insect/Pest Control—At least two elements are important in companion planting for insect control. Older plants with well developed aroma and essential oil accumulations should be used. You want the insects to know the plant is there. Second, it is important to use a large variety of herbs. Five different herbs help discourage the Cabbage Worm Butterfly, for instance, and one herb may work better than another in your area. Testing several herbs will help you determine the one that works best. The more unpleasant plants there are in the garden, the sooner harmful insects will get the idea that your garden is not a pleasant

Sow thistle grown with lettuce is one example of shallow/deep rooting symbiosis.

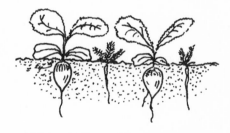

An example of using fast/slow maturing to advantage is to interplant carrots with radishes.

57. Also see Emanuel Epstein, "Roots", *Scientific American*, May, 1973, pp. 48-58.

58. Illegal in California, where it is considered a noxious weed which aggressively takes over cattle lands and prevents fodder from growing. It is probably also toxic to the cattle.

59. From the book, *How to Enjoy Your Weeds*, Audrey Wynne Hatfield, 1971, by Sterling Publishing Co., Inc., New York, ©1969 by Audrey Wynne Hatfield.

place to eat and propagate. The use of a large number of herbs also fits in with the diversity of plant life favored by nature. Much more research needs to be performed to determine the optimum ages for control plants and number of control plants per bed which provides optimum control. Too few plants will not control an insect problem and too many may reduce your yields. Some insect controls are:

☐ *White flies;* Marigolds (but not Pot Marigold (Calendula) and Flowering Tobacco. The first is supposed to excrete substances from its roots which are absorbed by the other plants. When the White Flies suck on the other plants, they think they are on a bad tasting marigold and leave. The Flowering Tobacco plant has a sticky substance on the underside of its leaves, where White Flies stick and die when they come there for a meal.

☐ *Ants;* Spearmint, Tansy and Pennyroyal. (Mint often attracts White Flies so you may want to grow a few Marigolds around for control, but not so many as to possibly impair the taste of the mint and certainly not one of the more poisonous Marigolds. This is another area for compromise. A few insects are probably less of a problem than mint with a strange taste.)

☐ *Nematodes and Root Pests*—Mexican Marigold (*Tagetes minuta*) "eliminates all kinds of destructive eelworms...wireworms, millepedes and various root eating pests from its vicinity". The French marigold, *Tagetes patula,* eliminates some "plant-destroying nematodes...at up to a range of three feet... The beneficial...eelworms which do not feed on healthy roots were not affected".[60]

☐ *Aphids—Yellow* Nasturtiums are a *decoy* for Black Aphids. They may be planted at the base of tomatoes for this purpose. Remove the plants and aphids before the insects begin to produce young with wings. Spearmint, Stinging Nettle, Southernwood and Garlic also help repel aphids.

☐ *Tomato Worms*—Borage reportedly helps repel tomato worms and/or serves as a decoy. It also attracts bees.

☐ *Gophers*—Elderberry cuttings placed in gopher holes and runs reportedly repel these animals. Daffodils, castor beans and *Euphorbia lathyrus* are all poisonous to gophers. Be careful, with the latter two, however, as they are also *very* toxic to children.

Birds, Bees & Animals—Sow Thistle attracts birds. Some are vegetarian and some are omnivorous. The omnivorous birds may stay for a main course of insects after a seed snack. If you are having trouble with birds eating the berries in your berry patch you could erect a wren house in the middle of it. Wrens are insectivores and they will not bother the berries. But they will attack any bird, however large, that comes near the nest.

Hummingbirds are attracted to red flowers. They especially like the tiny red, torch-like flowers of the Pineapple Sage in our garden. Bees may be attracted by Hyssop, Thyme, Catnip,

Birds and plants can work together too. The *sonchus* plant seeds attract the finch which afterwards eats aphids from the cabbage.

60. Ibid, p. 17.

Lemon Balm, Pot Marjoram, Sweet Basil, Summer Savory, Borage, Mint and *blue* flowers. Once in the garden they help pollinate.

Animals are good for the garden. Their manures can be used as fertilizers. Chickens are one of the few reliable controllers of earwigs, sowbugs, pill bugs, snails, grasshoppers, and maggots, though you may have to protect young seedlings from chickens pecking tasty plant morsels.

Companion planting in all its aspects can be a complex and often mind boggling exercise—if you worry too much about the details. Nature is complex and we can only assist and approximate her in our creations. If we are gentle in relation to her forces and balances, she can correct our errors and fill in for our lack of understanding. As you gain more experience, sensitivity and feeling, more companion planting details will come naturally. Don't let too much thinking spoil the fun and excitement of working with nature!

A LIST OF COMMON GARDEN VEGETABLES, THEIR COMPANIONS AND THEIR ANTAGONISTS[61]

Asparagus	Tomatoes, parsley, basil	
Beans	Potatoes, carrots, cucumbers, cauliflower, cabbage, summer savory, most other vegetables and herbs	Onions, garlic, gladiolus
Bush Beans	Potatoes, cucumbers, corn strawberries, celery, summer savory	Onions
Pole Beans	Corn, summer savory	Onions, beets, kohlrabi, sunflowers
Beets	Onions, kohlrabi	Pole Beans
Cabbage Family (Cabbage, cauliflower, kale, kohlrabi, broccoli)	Aromatic plants, potatoes celery, dill, camomile, sage, peppermint, rosemary, beets, onions	Strawberries, tomatoes, pole beans
Carrots	Peas, leaf lettuce, chives, onions, leeks, rosemary, sage, tomatoes	Dill
Celery	Leeks, tomatoes, bush beans cauliflower, cabbage	
Chives	Carrots	Peas, beans

61. From *Organic Gardening and Farming*, February, 1972, p. 54.

Corn	Potatoes, peas, beans cucumbers, pumpkins, squash	
Cucumbers	Beans, corn, peas, radishes, sunflowers	Potatoes, aromatic herbs
Eggplant	Beans	
Leeks	Onions, celery, carrots	
Lettuce	Carrots and radishes (lettuce, carrots and radishes make a strong team grown together), strawberries, cucumbers	
Onions (and garlic)	Beets, strawberries, tomatoes, lettuce, summer savory, camomile (sparsely)	Peas, beans
Parsley	Tomatoes, asparagus	
Peas	Carrots, turnips, radishes, cucumbers, corn, beans, most vegetables and herbs	Onions, garlic, gladiolus, potatoes
Potatoes	Beans, corn, cabbage, horse-radish (should be planted at corners of patch), marigold, eggplant (as a lure for Colorado potato beetle)	Pumpkins, squash, cucumbers, sunflowers, tomatoes, raspberries
Pumpkins	Corn	Potatoes
Radishes	Peas, nasturtiums, lettuce, cucumbers	
Soybeans	Grows with anything, helps everything	
Spinach	Strawberries	
Squash	Nasturtiums, corn	
Strawberries	Bush beans, spinach, borage, lettuce (as a border)	Cabbage
Sunflowers	Cucumbers	Potatoes
Tomatoes	Chives, onions, parsley, asparagus, marigolds, nasturtiums, carrots	Kohlrabi, potatoes, fennel, cabbage
Turnips	Peas	

A COMPANIONATE HERBAL FOR THE ORGANIC GARDEN[62]

A list of herbs, their companions, their uses, including some beneficial weeds and flowers.

Basil
: Companion to tomatoes, dislikes rue intensely. Improves growth and flavor. Repels flies and mosquitoes.

Beebalm
: Companion to tomatoes; improves growth and flavor.

Borage
: Companion to tomatoes, squash and strawberries; deters tomato worm; improves growth and flavor.

Caraway
: Plant here and there; loosens soil.

Catnip
: Plant in borders; deters flea beetle.

Camomile
: Companion to cabbage and onions; improves growth and flavor.

Chervil
: Companion to radishes; improves growth and flavor.

Chives
: Companion to carrots; improves growth and flavor.

Dead Nettle
: Companion to potatoes; deters potato bug; improves growth and flavor.

Dill
: Companion to cabbage; dislikes carrots; improves growth and health of cabbage.

Fennel
: Plant away from gardens. Most plants dislike it.

Flax
: Companion to carrots, potatoes; deters potato bug, improves growth and flavor.

Garlic
: Plant near roses and raspberries; deters Japanese beetles; improves growth and health.

Horseradish
: Plant at corners of potato patch to deter potato bug.

Henbit
: General insect repellent.

Hyssop
: Deters cabbage moth; companion to cabbage and grapes. Keep away from radishes.

Lamb's Quarters
: This edible weed should be allowed to grow in moderate amounts in the garden, especially in corn.

Lemon Balm
: Sprinkle throughout garden.

Lovage
: Improves flavor and health of plants if planted here and there.

Marigolds
: The workhorse of the pest deterrents. Plant throughout garden; it discourages Mexican bean beetles, nematodes and other insects.

62. From *Organic Gardening and Farming,* February, 1972, pp. 52 and 53.

Mint	Companion to cabbage and tomatoes; improves health and flavor; deters white cabbage moth.
Marjoram	Here and there in garden; improves flavors.
Mole Plant	Deters moles and mice if planted here and there.
Nasturtium	Companion to radishes, cabbage and cucurbits*; plant under fruit trees. Deters aphids, squash bugs, striped pumpkin beetles. Improves growth and flavor.
Petunia	Protects beans.
Pot Marigold	Companion to tomatoes, but plant elsewhere in garden too. Deters asparagus beetle, tomato worm and general garden pests.
Purslane	This edible weed makes good ground cover in the corn.
Pigweed	One of the best weeds for pumping nutrients from the subsoil, it is good for potatoes, onions and corn. Keep weeds thinned.
Peppermint	Planted among cabbages, it repels the white cabbage butterfly.
Rosemary	Companion to cabbage, beans carrots and sage; deters cabbage moth, bean beetles and carrot fly.
Rue	Keep it far away from Sweet Basil; plant near roses and raspberries; deters Japanese beetle.
Sage	Plant with rosemary, cabbage and carrots; keep away from cucumbers. Deters cabbage moth, carrot fly.
Southernwood	Plant here and there in garden; companion to cabbage, improves growth and flavor; deters cabbage moth.
Sowthistle	This weed in moderate amounts can help tomatoes, onions and corn.
Summer Savory	Plant with beans and onions; improves growth and flavor. Deters bean beetles.
Tansy	Plant under fruit trees; companion to roses and raspberries. Deters flying insects, Japanese beetles, striped cucumber beetles, squash bugs, ants.
Tarragon	Good throughout garden.
Thyme	Here and there in garden. It deters cabbage worm.
Valerian	Good anywhere in garden.
Wild Morning Glory**	Allow it to grow in corn.

Wormwood   As a border, it keeps animals from the garden.

Yarrow   Plant along borders, paths, near aromatic herbs; enhances
                                  essential oil production.

*Plants in the gourd family.

**We discourage the growing of wild morning glory anywhere in your garden, since it is a pernicious weed. Cultured morning glory is fine, however.

This information was collected from many sources, most notably the Bio-Dynamic Association and the herb Society of America.

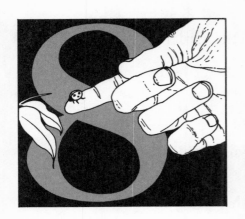

A Balanced Natural Backyard Ecosystem and Insect Life

I nsects and people are only one part of the complex, inter-related world of life. Both are important, integral parts of its living dynamism. Insects are an important part of the diet for many birds, toads, frogs and other insects in nature's complex food chain. With the biodynamic/French intensive method comes a realization that every time you relate to an insect you are relating with the whole system of life, and that, if you choose to dominate the insect world system of life, rather than work in harmony with it, part of the system dies. For example, we depend on insects for pollination of many of our vegetables, fruits, flowers, herbs, fibers and cover crops. When we choose dominating, death-oriented control, then the scope and depth of our life becomes narrower and smaller. So, in reality, we are detracting from our own lives rather than adding to them. In trying to isolate an insect and deal with it separately out of relation to the ecosystem in which it lives, we work against the whole life support system, which in turn works against us in counterproductive results.

When an excess of insects appears in a garden, nature is indicating a problem exists in the life of that garden. In each case, we need to become sensitive to the source of the imbalance. Observation and gentle action will produce the best results. In contrast, when poisons are used, beneficial predators are killed as well as the targeted harmful insects. Spraying trees to eliminate worms or beetles often results in a secondary outbreak of spider mites or aphids because ladybugs and other predators cannot reestablish themselves as quickly as the destructive species.

Paying attention to the soil and plant health, planning a varied environment, and leaving a few wild spaces for unexpected benefactors minimizes pest losses more effectively than the use of poisons. Also, in order to have beneficial insects in your food producing area, there must be their food—some of the harmful ones! If there are no harmful insects, then there will be few, if any, beneficial insects ready to act as a seed population of friendly guardians. This seeming paradox—the presences of both kinds of insects for the most healthy garden—is symbolic of nature's balances. Not too much moisture, but enough. Not too much aeration, but enough. Not too many harmful insects, but enough. You find the need for these balances everywhere—in the compost pile, in the soil in the mini-climate, and in the backyard micro-cosm as a whole.

In a small backyard garden ecosystem or mini-farm it is especially important to welcome all life forms as much as possible. Ants destroy fruitfly and housefly larvae and keep the garden cleaned of rotting debris. Have you ever squashed a snail and watched how the ants come to whisk the remains away almost within a day? Earwigs are carnivorous and prey on other insects. Tachinid flies parasitize caterpillars, earwigs, tomato worms, and grasshoppers to lay their eggs in them. We've found cabbage worms immobilized and bristling with cottony white torpedoes the size of a pinhead: larvae of the braconid wasp which will hatch and go in search of more cabbage worms. Toads eat earwigs, slugs and other pests. Chickens control earwigs, sowbugs and flies. Even the ancient, but fascinating, snails have a natural predator: humans!

The first step in insect control is to cultivate strong vigorous plants by cultivating a healthy place in which they can grow. Normally (about 90% of the time), insects only attack unhealthy plants. Just as a healthy person who eats good food is less susceptible to disease, so are healthy plants that are on a good diet less susceptible to plant diseases and insect attack. It is *not* the insect which is the source of the problem, but rather an unhealthy soil. The soil needs your energy, not the insect. The uninterrupted growth stressed by the biodynamic/French intensive method is also important to the maintenance of plant health. In short, we are shepherds providing the conditions our plants need for healthy, vigorous growth.

Some elements to consider:

☐ is the soil being dug properly

☐ are the proper plant nutriments available in the soil

☐ is enough compost being used

☐ is the soil pH within reasonable limits for the plant being grown

☐ are the seedlings being transplanted properly

☐ are the plants being watered properly

☐ is weeding being done effectively

☐ is the soil being maintained in a way which will enable it to retain moisture and nutriments

☐ are the plants receiving enough sun

☐ are the plants being grown in season.

Another method of providing for plant health and for minimizing insect and disease problems is to keep a correct balance of phosphorous and potash in the soil in relation to the amount of nitrogen present. (See page 26.) The optimal ratio among these elements is still to be determined. Research also needs to be completed to determine the minimum amounts of these elements (in pounds per 100 square feet) which should be in the soil. (Smaller amounts of organic fertilizer elements are required, since they break down more slowly and remain available to the plants for a longer period of time.)

Proper planning of the garden can eliminate many insect and disease problems!

☐ Use seeds which grow well in your climate and soil.

☐ Use plant varieties which are hardy, insect resistant, and disease resistant. New strains, especially hybrids (whether developed for higher yields, disease resistance or other reasons) should usually be avoided. Hybrids often produce food of lower nutritive value in comparison with older strains and often use up nutriment from the soil at a more rapid rate than the rate at which a living soil can produce nutriment. Hybrids are also often very susceptible to a few diseases even when they are greatly resistant to many prevalent ones.

☐ Companion plant: grow vegetables and flowers together that grow well with each other.

☐ Normally, do not put the same vegetable in the same growing bed each year. This practice invites disease.

☐ Rotate your crops: follow heavy feeders with heavy givers and then light feeders.

Encourage natural insect control by enlisting the aid of nature:

Birds—some are vegetarians. Others are omnivorous. A bird which stops for a seed snack may remain for an insect dinner. A house wren feeds 500 spiders and caterpillars to her young in one afternoon, a brown thrasher consumes 6,000 insects a day, a chickadee eats 138,000 canker worm eggs in 25 days and a pair of flickers eat 5,000 ants as a snack. A baltimore oriole can comsume 17 hairy caterpillars a minute. The presence of birds may be encouraged by the use of moving water, the planting of

63. Beatrice Trum Hunter, *Gardening Without Poisons*, Berkeley Publishing Corp., New York, 1971, pp. 31, 37, 42, 43, 48. The Berkeley Edition was published by arrangement with the Houghton Mifflin Company, who are the original publishers of *Gardening Without Poisons*.

bushes for their protection, the planting of sour berry bushes for food and the growing of plants that have seeds the birds like to eat.

Toads, Snakes and Spiders—also eat insects and other garden pests. Toads eat as many as 10,000 insects in three months including cutworms, slugs, crickets, ants, caterpillars and squash bugs.

Lady Bugs—are good predators since they eat one particular pest, aphids, and do not eat beneficial insects. Ladybugs eat 40-50 insects per day and their larvae eat even more.

Praying Mantids—are predators which should only be used in infestation emergencies, since they eat beneficial as well as harmful insects. They are not selective and even eat each other.

Trichogramma Wasps—lay their eggs in hosts such as moth and butterfly larvae which eat leaves. When they hatch, the wasp larvae parasitize the host larvae, which fail to reach maturity. Up to 98 percent of the hosts are rendered useless in this way.

Tachinid Flies—are parasites which help control caterpillars, Japanese beetles, earwigs, gypsy moths, brown tail moths, tomato worms and grasshoppers.

Syrphid Flies—are parasites that prey upon aphids and help pollinate crops.

After you have done everything possible to provide a healthy, balanced garden for your plants, you may still have insect problems. If so, you should approach the insects involved with the idea of *living control* rather than elimination. Minimization of the pest allows dynamic living control to occur: beneficial predators need the harmful insects as a food source. Total elimination of the insect would disrupt nature's balances.

If there is a problem, identify the pest and try to determine if an *environmental change* can solve the problem. In our research garden, we have minimized (not eliminated though!) gophers by introducing gopher snakes.

The pocket Golden Guides on *Insects* and *Insect Pests* are invaluable guides for getting to know the creatures that inhabit your garden with you. Out of the 86,000 species of insect in the United States, 76,000 are considered beneficial or friendly.[64] So be careful! An insect which looks ugly or malicious may be a friend. If you can't seem to find an obvious culprit, try exploring at night with a flashlight. Many are active then.

Ask yourself if the *damage* is *extensive* enough to warrant a "policing" effort. During 1972 bush beans were grown in one of our test beds. The primary leaves were almost entirely destroyed by the 12-spotted cucumber beetle. But in most cases the damage was not so rapid as to prevent the development of

64. *Ibid, p. 28.*

healthy secondary leaves. The less tender secondary leaves were ultimately attacked and became quite heavily eaten. About 80 percent of the secondary leaf area remained, however, and very tasty, unblemished beans were harvested. The yield in pounds was still 3.9 times the United States average! Recent tests have shown that leaf damage of up to 30% by insects can actually increase the yield of some crops. At another extreme you may wish to sacrifice some yield for beauty: many destructive caterpillars become beautiful butterflies. To get the yield you want and/or to encourage the presence of butterflies, you can plant extra plants of the crop they like.

We often underestimate the ability of plants to take care of themselves. The damage done by insects is often a very small percentage of the edible crop. Because of this, many biodynamic gardeners plant a little extra for the insect world to eat. This practice is beautiful, mellow and in keeping with life-giving forms of insect control. Furthermore, extensive research has shown that beneficial organisms found in soil and ocean environments can withstand stress, in the form of temperature, pressure, pH and nutriment fluctuations, to a much greater degree in an organically fertilized medium than in a synthetically fertilized medium. I suspect researchers will come to a similar conclusion about plant resistance to insect attack.

Any time an insect or other pest invades your garden, there is an opportunity to learn more about nature's cycles and balances. Learn why they are there and find a *living control*. Look for controls that will affect only the one harmful insect. Protect new seedlings from birds and squirrels with netting or chicken wire, trap earwigs in dry dark places, wash aphids off with a strong spray of water, or block ants with a sticky barrier of vaseline, tanglefoot or tack trap. While you are doing this, continue to strive for a long-term natural balance in your growing area.

At our Common Ground Research Garden the only two pest problems we have had to put a lot of energy into are snails and gophers. The first few years we primarily trapped gophers. A lot of time was spent checking and resetting traps and worrying about them, yet the damage they did was probably only about 5%. We later found that in addition to gopher snakes they really don't like smelly things down their holes (sardines, garlic juice, fish heads, male urine, and dead gophers). Here a combination of approaches and gentle persistance has paid off. Gopher snakes are, of course, the best preventers of a population explosion. Finally, we noticed that the gophers come mainly from a grassy area east of the garden. We hope to eventually block that side with a wide bed of daffodils. Daffodils contain arsenic in their bulbs and thereby can discourage these animals.

We have a simple routine for snails and slugs. At the end of the spring rains we go out at night with flashlights and collect gallons of them. The snails are then dropped in buckets of soapy water which will kill them. If you use soap that is quick to degrade, they can be dumped on the compost pile the next day. Most of them are caught in the first three nights. Going out occasionally over the next two weeks catches new ones that were too small in the first sweep or which have just hatched from eggs laid in the soil. Such a concentrated cleanup can be effective for several months.

Another kind of problem has been solved through observation. For example, one year a cherry tomato bed was wilting. Several people, including a graduate student studying insects, told us it was caused by nematodes. When we dug down into the soil to look for the damage, we discovered the real source. The soil was bone dry below the upper eight inches. A good soaking took care of the problem and we learned to be more careful about watering so the beds would not dry out. Most important, we have learned not to take gardening advice on faith, but to always check it out for ourselves—as we hope you will.

Some other living control approaches to try are:

Hand-picking the insects from the plants once you are certain the insect involved is *harmful* and the source of the problem. Consult a book, such as *Insect Pests* (see Bibliography), which has color drawings of insects in their several stages (nymph, larva, adult). An insect is often harmful in only one stage and can even be beneficial in others.

Spraying. In general, insects may be divided into two categories—those which chew and bite plants and those which suck juices from them. *Chewing or biting insects*, include caterpillars, flea beetles, potato bugs, cankerworms, cutworms, and grasshoppers. *Aromatic and distasteful* substances such as garlic, onion and pepper sprays can discourage them. *Sucking Insects* include aphids, thrips, nymphs of the squash bug, flies and scale insects. Soap solutions (not detergents which would damage the plant and soil as well as the insects), clear miscible oil solutions and other solutions which asphyxiate the insects by coating their tender bodies and preventing respiration through body spiracles or breathing holes, help control these insects.

Traps, such as shredded newspaper in clay pots turned upside down on sticks in the garden, will attract earwigs during daylight hours. Snails and slugs can be trapped under damp boards. They retreat to these places in the heat and light of the day.

Barriers, such as the sticky commercial Tanglefoot substance, will catch some insects crawling along tree trunks during part of their life cycle. When insects are caught in this manner, infestation of the tree in a later season is often prevented. (Tanglefoot barriers must be applied to apple tree trunks in July to catch codling moth larvae leaving the tree. This will minimize

codling moth infestation the following spring. Plan ahead!) Plant barriers and decoys can also be used. Grow a vegetable or flower preferred by a particular insect away from the garden to attract it to another location. Place repellant plants near a vegetable or flower that needs protection.

You may also wish to plant some herbs in your beds for insect control. The age and number of plants used per 100 square feet determine the herb's effectiveness. A young plant does not have an aroma or root exudate strong enough to discourage harmful insects or to attract beneficial ones. Similarly, too few herbs will not control a pest or attract a needed predator. Too many herbs may retard vegetable growth and yield. Composite flowers, such as Pot Marigolds (Calendulas), are excellent attractants for predatory insects because their large supplies of pollen serve as predator food sources. A few (2-4) plants per 100 square foot bed will probably suffice. We have not done a lot of experiments with them yet, however, since accurate testing can take two to three years for one herb grown with one food plant to control one insect. This requires more time and funding than we have. You may wish to try some of these biodynamic observations though. It's a lot of fun to try and see for yourself!

INSECT PESTS AND PLANT CONTROLS[65]

Insect Pest	Plant Control
Ants	— Spearmint, Tansy, Pennyroyal
Aphids	— Nasturtium, Spearmint, Stinging Nettle, Southernwood, Garlic
Mexican Bean Beetle	— Potatoes
Black Fly	— Intercropping, Stinging Nettle
Cabbage Worm Butterfly	— Sage, Rosemary, Hyssop, Thyme, Mint, Wormwood, Southernwood
Striped Cucumber Beetle	— Radish
Cutworm	— Oak leaf mulch, Tanbark
Black Flea Beetle	— Wormwood, Mint
Flies	— Nut Trees, Rue, Tansy, spray of Wormwood and/or Tomato
June Bug Grub	— Oak leaf mulch, Tanbark
Japanese Beetle	— White Geranium, Datura
Plant Lice	— Castor Bean, Sassafras, Pennyroyal
Mosquito	— Legumes
Malaria Mosquito	— Wormwood, Southernwood, Rosemary
Moths	— Sage, Santolina, Lavender, Mint, Stinging Nettle, Herbs
Colorado Potato Beetle	— Eggplant, Flax, Green Beans
Potato Bugs	— Flax, Eggplant
Slugs	— Oak leaf mulch, Tanbark
Squash Bugs	— Nasturtium

Weevils	— Garlic
Wooly Aphis	— Nasturtium
Worms in Goats	— Carrots
Worms in Horses	— Tansy leaves, Mulberry leaves

65. Helen Philbrick and Richard B. Gregg, *Companion Plants and How to Use Them*, The Devin-Adair Company, Old Greenwich, Connecticut, 1966, pp. 52-53. This book and others should be consulted for the proper use and application rates of these plant remedies. Improper use or application can cause problems and could be harmful to you, your plants and animals.

Probably the most important form of insect control with plants is just diverse cropping. The biodynamic/French intensive method uses diverse cropping and we have only experienced 5 to 10 percent crop loss due to pests when we are performing "the method" properly. Biodynamic gardeners and farmers also use diverse cropping and have suggested that one plant 10 percent more area to make up for crop losses. In contrast the monocropped acreage of today's commercial agriculture provides an ideal uniform habitat for widespread attack by pests which favor a single crop. Pesticides have been recommended to counteract the problem inherent in monocropping. Yet, the Environmental Protection Agency estimates "that thirty years ago American farmers used 50 million pounds of pesticides and lost 7 percent of their crop before harvest. Today, farmers use twelve times more pesticides yet the percentage of the crops lost before harvest has almost doubled."[66] In fact, many pesticides targeted for one pest species actually cause increases in the numbers of non-targeted pests. By their action on the physiology of the plant, pesticides can make a plant more nutritionally favorable to insects, thereby increasing the fertility and longevity of feeding pests.[67]

It is becoming more evident that pesticides are not an effective solution for crop loss due to pests. It seems that *diverse* cropping without pesticides may be able to reduce total pest losses more than monocropping with pesticides, even in large-scale agriculture. Using standard agricultural practices, Cornell University researchers, in a five-year study completed in 1970, found that without pesticides the insect population could be cut in half when only two crops were grown together.[68] You will make this, and even more, possible when you grow plants in your backyard with life-giving techniques!

Only a brief introduction to insect control has been given here. An emphasis has been placed on philosophy and general approaches. *The Bug Book, Companion Plants* and *Gardening*

66. See James S. Turner, *A Chemical Feast: Report on the Food and Drug Administration* (Ralph Nader Study Group Reports) New York: Grossman, 1970 cited in *Food First*, by Frances Moore Lappe and Joseph Collins, Boston: Houghton Mifflin Company, 1977, p. 49.

67. Francis Chaboussou, "The Role of Potassium and of Cation Equilibrium in the Resistance of the Plant," Chaboussou is the Director of Research at the French National Institute for Agricultural Research, Agricultural Zoology Station of the South-West, 22 PONT DE LA MAYE, FRANCE.

68. See Jeff Cox, "The Technique That Halves Your Insect Population", *Organic Gardening and Farming*, May, 1973, pp. 103-104.

Without Poisons (see Bibliography) have already vigorously explored in detail the spectrum of organic insect control. These books give companion planting combinations, recipes for insect control solutions, and addresses from which predatory insects can be obtained.

I hope each person who reads this book will try at least one, small, 3 foot by 3 foot biodynamic/French intensive growing bed. You should find the experience fun and exciting beyond your wildest expectations!

Bibliography

Books marked with an * may be mail-ordered from Ecology Action, 2225 El Camino Real, Palo Alto, CA 94306. Write for current prices and to enquire about other titles. Ecology Action publishes several research papers on the biodynamic/French intensive method and has books and information on beekeeping, mini-farming, homesteading and related topics.

Bed Preparation

Sunset, "Getting Started with the French Intensive Method," September, 1972, p. 168.

Companion Planting

*Helen Philbrick and Richard B. Gregg, *Companion Plants and How to Use Them*, The Devin-Adair Company, Old Greenwich, Connecticut, 1966, 113 pp.

Evelyn Speiden Gregg, *Herb Chart*, Biodynamic Farming and Gardening Assoc., Wyoming, Rhode Island. Detailed cultural notes.

*Juliette de Bairacli Levy, *The Herbal Handbook for Farm and Stable*, Faber and Faber, London. Rodale Press, Emmaus, PA, 1976, 320 pp.

*Audrey Wynne Hatfield, *How to Enjoy Your Weeds*, Sterling Publishing Company, New York, 1971, 192 pp. Delightful. Includes an herbal lawn, flower salads and other charming ideas.

Peter Tomkins and Christopher Bird, "Love Among the Cabbages," Harpers, November, 1972, pp. 90ff. *The Secret Life of Plants*, Harper and Row, 1972, 402 pp. Fascinating.

Emanual Epstein, "Roots," Scientific American, May, 1973, pp. 48-58.

Charles Morrow Wilson, *Roots: Miracles Below*, Doubleday, 1968, 234 pp.

*Alexander C. Martin, *Weeds*, Golden Press, New York, 160 pp. Inexpensive identification guide.

*Ehrenfried E. Pfeiffer, *Weeds and What They Tell*, Biodynamic Farming and Gardening Association, Wyoming, Rhode Island, 1970, 96 pp. Reading soil conditions by the weeds.

*Joseph A. Cocannouer, *Weeds: Guardians of the Soil*, Devin-Adair, New York, 1948. 179 pp. How weeds help your garden.

John E. Weaver and William E. Bruner, *Root Development of Vegetable Crops*, McGraw Hill, New York, 1927, 351 pp. Excellent diagrams of root systems.

Composting

Composting for the Tropics, Henry Doubleday Research Association, Bocking, England, March, 1963, 28 pp. Useful pamphlet for humid areas

Gary Soucie, "How You Gonna Keep It Down on The Farm," *Audubon*, September, 1972, pp. 112-115.

William C. Denison, "Life in Tall Trees," *Scientific American*, June, 1973, pp. 75-80

Jeff Cox, "What You Should Know About Nitrogen," *Organic Gardening and Farming*, June, 1972, pp. 69-74. See insert on page 68, also.

*Clarence G. Golueke, *Composting: A Study of the Process and Its Principles*. Rodale Press, Emmaus, Pennsylvania, 1972, 110 pp. For those with an advanced interest.

*H. H. Koepf, *Compost*. Biodynamic Farming and Gardening Association, 1966, 18 pp. Short detailed pamphlet.

Richard Alther and Richard O. Raymond, *Improving Garden Soil with Green Manures*, Garden Way Publishing, Charlotte, Vermont, 1974. 44 pp. Contains good 2-page chart.

Experiences

Ann Zwinger, *Beyond the Aspen Grove*, Random House, New York, 1970, 368 pp.

*Helen and Scott Nearing, *Living the Good Life*, Schocken Books, New York, 1970, 213 pp.

Louis Bromfield, *Malabar Farm*, Ballantine Books, New York, 1970, 470 pp.

Kenneth McNeill Wells, *The Owl Pen Reader*, Doubleday and Co., Garden City, New York, 1969, 445 pp.

Edwin Way Teale (Ed.), *The Wilderness World of John Muir*, Houghton Mifflin Company, Boston, 1964, 332 pp.

Flowers

Audrey Wynne Hatfield, *Flowers to Know and Grow*, Charles Scribners Sons, New York, 1950, 174 pp.

Anthony Huxley (Ed.) *Garden Annuals and Bulbs*, The MacMillan Company, New York, 1971, 208 pp. *Garden Perennials and Water Plants*, the MacMillan Company, New York, 1971, 216 pp.

The Oxford Book of Garden Flowers, Oxford University Press, 1963, 207 pp.

Sunset Western Garden Book, By the Editors of Sunset Magazine and Sunset Books, Lane Magazine & Book Co., Menlo Park, CA 1970, 448 pp. Indispensible descriptions and cultural directions for flowering plants, trees, and landscaping. For West Coast gardeners. Not organic.

*Catharine Osgood Foster, *Organic Flower Gardening*, Rodale Press, Emmaus, Pennsylvania, 1975, 305 pp. Excellent!

Food & Nutrition

*Mollie Katzen, *The Moosewood Cookbook*. Ten Speed Press, Berkeley, Calif., 1977, 221 pp. Tasty recipes for lots of fresh vegetables.

12 Months Harvest. Ortho Book Division, Chevron Chemical Co., San Francisco, 1975, 96 pp. Covers canning, freezing, smoking, drying, cheese, cider, soap and grinding grain. Many good tips.

Agricultural Research Service, United States Department of Agriculture, *Composition of Foods*, Agriculture Handbook No. 8, U.S. Government Printing Office, Washington, D.C., 1963, 190 pp.

*Gen Macmaniman, *Dry It*, Living Food Dehydrators, Fall City, Washington, 1973, 58 pp.

Maria C. Linder, "A Review of the Evidence for Food Quality", *Bio-Dynamics*, Summer 1973, pp. 1-11.

*Carol Stoner, *Stocking Up*, Rodale Press, Inc., Book Division, Emmaus, Pennsylvania, 1973, 351 pp.

General

*Sir Albert Howard, *The Soil and Health*, Devin-Adair, New York, 1956, 307 pp. A cornerstone of the organic movement.

*Rudolf Steiner, *Agriculture—A Course of Eight Lectures*, Biodynamic Agricultural Assoc., London, 1958, 175 pp. The basis of the bio-dynamic movement. Advanced reading.

Michael J. Perelman and Kevin P. Shea, "The Big Farm," *Environment*, December, 1972, pp. 10-15

*Robert Rodale (Ed.), *The Basic Book of Organic Gardening*, Balantine Books, New York, 1971, 377 pp. Condensed information includes 14-day compost and nationwide planting dates.

*J. I. Rodale (Ed.) *The Encyclopedia of Organic Gardening*, and *How To Grow Vegetables and Fruits by the Organic Method*, Rodale Books, Emmaus, Pennsylvania, 1959 and 1961, 1145 pp. and 926 pp. respectively. Two excellent references. Many prefer the encyclopedia format but we find the second to be more complete.

Joseph A. Cocannouer, *Farming With Nature*, University of Oklahoma Press, Norman, Oklahoma, 1954, 147 pp.

F. H. King, *Farmers of Forty Centuries*, Rodale Press, Inc., Emmaus, Pennsylvania, 1972, 441 pp. First-hand observations of Chinese agriculture.

Michael J. Perelman, "Farming With Petroleum," *Environment*, October, 1972, pp. 8-13

Anne Pratt, *Flowering Plants, Grasses, Sedges and Ferns of Great Britain*, Frederick Warne and Co., London, 1905, 4 vols.

Thomas Smith, *French Gardening*, Utopia Press, London, 1909, 128 pp.

*John and Helen Philbrick, *Gardening for Health and Nutrition*, Rudolf Steiner Publications, Blauvelt, New York, 1971, 93 pp.

*James Edward Knott, *Handbook for Vegetable Growers*, John Wiley and Sons, Inc., N.Y. 1957, 245 pp. Useful charts for small farmers. Heavy chemical orientation.

William Bronson, "The Lesson of a Garden," *Cry California*, Winter, '70/'71.

John C. Jeavons, "New Ways from Old," *Cry California*, Winter '73/'74.

Bargyla and Gylver Rateaver, *The Organic Method Primer*, published by the authors, Pauma Valley, California, 92061, 1973, 257 pp. Packed with detailed information.

*Alice Heckel (Ed.) *The Pfeiffer Garden Book—Biodynamics in the Home Garden*, Biodynamic Farming and Gardening Association, Wyoming, Rhode Island, 1967, 199 pp.

*Richard Merrill (Ed.), *Radical Agriculture*, Harper and Row, New York, 1976, 459 pp. Philosophical and political aspects of food production.

*John Seymour, *The Complete Book of Self-Sufficiency*, Faber & Faber, London, England, 1976, 256 pp. Coffee-table size *The Self-Sufficient Gardener*, Faber & Faber, London, England, 1978, 256 pp. Coffee-table size Seymour has long been a popular back-to-the-land advocate in England, both doing it and writing about it in his own humorous style. His new "productions" are gorgeously illustrated, accurate and uncluttered. The first includes grains, livestock, energy, and skills such as spinning, metalwork and thatching as well as raising fruits and vegetables. The second listed concentrates on smaller-scale food production.

John Seymour, *I'm A Stranger Here Myself*, Faber & Faber, 1978, 140 pp. Absorbing personal account.

*Catharine Osgood Foster, *The Organic Gardener*, Random House, New York, 1972, 234 pp. Excellent, chatty, experienced. New England area especially.

Ken and Pat Kraft, *Growing Food the Natural Way*, Doubleday, New York, 1973, 292 pp. California-area orientation.

*Jamie Jobb, *My Garden Companion*, Sierra Club, San Francisco, 1977, 350 pp. Especially for beginners.

*Wolf Storl, *Culture and Horticulture*. To be republished in 1979 by the Bio-dynamic Farming and Gardening Assoc., Wyoming, Rhode Island. Bio-dynamics and organic agricultural history explained simply.

Lady E. B. Balfour, *The Living Soil* and *The Haughley Experiment*, Faber and Faber, London, 1943 and 1975, 383 pp.

*Tom Cuthbertson, *Alan Chadwick's Enchanted Garden*, E. P. Dutton, New York, 1978, 199 pp. Captures the flavor of working under the originator of the biodynamic/French intensive method.

*Wendell Berry, *The Unsettling of America: Culture and Agriculture*. Sierra Club, San Francisco, 1977, 226 pp. Eloquent and passionate view of the sociological aspects of farming.

Edward Hyams, *Soil and Civilization.* Harper & Row, New York, 1976, 312 pp. Reprint from 1952.

Vernon Gill Carter and Tom Dale, *Topsoil & Civilization*, University of Oklahoma Press, 1955, 292 pp. Norman, Oklahoma.

R. Dalziel O'Brien, *Intensive Gardening*, Faber & Faber, London, 1956, 183 pp. Useful for potential mini-farmers.

L. H. Bailey, *The Principles of Vegetable Gardening*, MacMillan, N.Y., 1901, 450 pp.
The Forcing Book, MacMillan, New York, 1903, 266 pp.
Manual of Gardening, MacMillan, New York, 1914, 541 pp.
The Farm and Garden Rule-Book, MacMillan, New York, 1915, 586 pp.

Greenhouses

J. L. H. Chase, *Cloche Gardening*, Faber & Faber, London, 1948, 195 pp.

*A. Aquatias, *Intensive Culture of Vegetables*, Solar Survival Press, Harrisville, New Hampshire, 03450, 1978, 192 pp. Reprint from 1913 on raising food under glass.

Helen and Scott Nearing, *Our Sun-Heated Greenhouse*, Garden Way, Charlotte, Vt., 1977, 148 pp.

Rick Fisher and Bill Yanda, *The Food and Heat Producing Solar Greenhouse*, John Muir Publications, Santa Fe, N.M. 87501, 1976, 161 pp. Detailed.

Insect Life

Fish and Wildlife Service, U.S. Department of the Interior, *Attracting and Feeding Birds*, Conservation Bulletin No. 1, U.S. Government Printing Office, Washington, D.C., revised 1973, 10 pp.

*John and Helen Philbrick (Eds.), *The Bug Book*, Garden Way Publishing, Charlotte, Vt., 1974, 126 pp.

*Robert T. Mitchell, *Butterflies and Moths*, Golden Press, New York, 1962, 160 pp.

*Beatrice Trum Hunter, *Gardening Without Poisons*, Berkeley Publishing, New York, 1971, 352 pp. Comprehensive survey of insect control methods.

*Herbert S. Zim, *Insects*, Golden Press, New York, 1956, 160 pp.

*George S. Fichter, *Insect Pests*, Golden Press, New York, 1966, 160 pp.

*Herbert W. Levi, *Spiders*, Golden Press, New York, 1968, 160 pp.

Seed Propagation

H. Garrison Wilkes and Susan Wilkes, "The Green Revolution," *Environment*, October, 1972, pp. 32-39.

Robert Johnston, Jr., *Growing Garden Seeds*, Johnny's Selected Seeds, Albion, Maine 04910, 1976, 32 pp. Culture of plants for saving seed.

Douglas C. Miller, *Vegetable & Herb Seed Growing for the Gardener and Small Farmer.* Bullkill Creek Publishing, Hersey Michigan, 1977, 46 pp. A good book to start with.

*Craig Dremann, *Vegetable Seed Production*, Redwood City Seed Co., Box 360, Redwood City, Calif., 94064, 1974, 6 pp. For moderate climates. Expanded version planned.

Seed Catalogs

Abundant Life Seeds, Box 30018, Seattle, WA 98103. Small seed exchange for residents of the Pacific Northwest and California only. 50¢.

Burpee Seed Co., Clinton, IA 52732. Large well-known company with wide selection of most vegetables and flowers.

DiGiorgi Co., Council Bluffs, Iowa 51501. Forage crops, old-fashioned lettuce and other vegetables, open-pollinated corn.

Epicure Seeds, Avon, New York, 14414. New but looks great. Choice varieties from gourmet seed houses of Europe.

Gurney's, Yankton, S.D. 57078. Unusual vegetables. Cold-weather vegetables and fruit trees.

Hart Seed Co., Wethersfield, Ct. 06109. Largest selection of old-fashioned and non-hybrid vegetables. Many hard-to-find varieties available on request.

J. L. Hudson Seed Co., P.O. Box 1058, Redwood City, CA 94064. One of the world's largest selection of flower and herb seeds. Catalog. 50¢

Johnny's Selected Seeds, Albion, ME 04910. Small seed company with integrity. Carries native American crops, select oriental vegetables, grains, short-maturing soybeans. Catalog: 50¢

Meadowbrook Herb Garden, Rt. 138, Wyoming, RI 02898. Bio-Dynamically grown spices, herbs, teas, and herb seeds.

Nichols Garden Nursery, 1190 North Pacific Hwy., Albany, Oregon 97321. Unusual specialties: elephant garlic, luffa sponge, winemaking supplies, herbs.

Park Seed Co., Greenwood, S.C. 29647. The best selection of flowers. Gorgeous, full-color catalog available free.

Redwood City Seed Co., P.O. Box 361, Redwood City, CA 94061. Basic selection of non-hybrid, untreated vegetable and herb seeds. Expert on locating various tree seeds, including redwoods. Catalog. 25¢.

R. H. Shumway, Rockford, Ill. 61101. Good selection of grains, fodders and cover crops.

Sassafras Farms, Box 1007, Topanga, CA 90290. Two dozen organically grown vegetables varieties and misc. roots. Send $1 for poster-catalog.

Stark Brothers, Louisiana, MO 63353. Specializes in fruit trees, especially dwarfs and semi-dwarfs. Carries many developed by Luther Burbank.

Stokes Seeds, Box 548, Buffalo, N.Y. 14240. Carries excellent varieties of many vegetables, especially carrots.

Suttons Seeds, London Road, Earley, Reading, Berkshire, RG6 1AB. For gourmet gardeners. Excellent, tasty varieties, hot-house vegetables

True Seed Exchange, R. R. 1, Princeton, MO 64673. Exchange for home-grown seed. To join (i.e. to list your own or receive listings) send $2.

Vilmorin-Andrieux, 4, quai de la Megisserie, 75001 Paris. Old, respected seed house specializing in high-quality gourmet vegetables. Catalog in French. Expensive minimum order.

Arthur Yates & Co., P.O. Box 72, Revesvy 2212, New South Wales, Australia. Specializes in tropical varieties suitable for the southern hemisphere. International seed catalog free.

Soil

Edward H. Faulkner, *Plowman's Folly*, University of Oklahoma Press, Norman, Oklahoma, 1943, 155 pp. Classic.

T. Lyttleton Lyon & Harry O. Buckman, *The Nature and Properties of Soils*, MacMillan, New York, 1929, 428 pp. First edition only for more organic treatment.

Peter Farb, *Living Earth*, Harper Colophon, New York, 1959, 175 pp. Easy-to-read peek at the life under the soil.

Handbook on Soils, Brooklyn Botanic Garden, Brooklyn, New York, 1956, 81 pp. Some photos of root systems in the soil.

Trees

S.R. Williams, *Compost Fruit Growing*, W. Foulsham and Co., Ltd., London, 1961, 126 pp.

*J. Russell Smith, *Tree Crops, Key to a Permanent Agriculture*, Devin-Adair, Old Greenwich, Conn., 1953, 408 pp. Classic work on an important concept.

*J. Sholto Douglas & Robert A. de J. Hart, *Forest Farming*, Watkins, London and Rodale Press, Emmaus, PA, 1976, 193 pp. Excellent.

L.H. Bailey, *The Pruning Manual*, MacMillan, New York, 1954, 320 pp. Constantly revised for 50 years and now out of print.

Reid Brooks and Claron Hesse, *Western Fruit Gradening*. University of California Press, Berkeley, CA, 1953, 287 pp. Old but still good.

Louis Lorette, *The Lorette System of Pruning*. Martin Hopkinson & Company Ltd., London, 1925, 164 pp. Still practiced by Chadwick. Fruit trees are gently pinched and trained during summer.

*Jean Giono, *The Man Who Planted Hope and Grew Happiness*. Friends of Nature, Winchester, Mass. 01890. 1967, 17 pp. True account of a one-man tree planting program. Inspirational.

Anthony Huxley (Ed.), *Deciduous Garden Trees and Shrubs*, MacMillan, New York, 1973, 216 pp.

Anthony Huxley (Ed.). *Evergreen Garden Trees and Shrubs*, MacMillan, New York, 1973, 216 pp.

Water

*Joseph A. Cocannouer, *Water and the Cycle of Life*. Devin-Adair, Old Greenwich, Conn., 1962, 142 pp. All his books are fascinating and easy to read.

Vegetables

The Oxford Book of Food Plants, Oxford University Press, 1969, 207 pp.

T. W. Sanders, *Vegetables and Their Cultivation*, Q. H. & L. Collingridge, London, 1928 (many editions), 508 pp.

*MM. Vilmorin-Andrieux, *The Vegetable Garden*, The Jeavons-Leler Press, Palo Alto, CA, 1976, 620 pp. Very detailed reprint of 1885 English edition by John Murray.

*Albert C. Burrage, *Burrage on Vegetables*, Houghton Mifflin, New York, 1975, 224 pp. Good notes on scheduling for continuous harvest.

Sutton and Sons, *The Culture of Vegetables and Flowers from Seeds and Roots*, Simpkin, Marshall, Hamilton, Kent & Co., London, 1898, 427 pp. Excellent, Out-of-Print.

Tools

Walt Nicke's Garden Talk, Box 667 G, Hudson, New York, 12534. Catalog of Haws watering cans and other high quality small tools.

Superbly crafted D-handled spades and forks from England may soon be available in this country. Write Ecology Action for information.

Who is Ecology Action?

Ecology Action of the Midpeninsula is a local, non-profit, tax-exempt, environmental research and education organization. Formed in the early 1970's, it acted as a catalyst in the recycling of glass and metal wastes in the city of Palo Alto, California. This project, for which Ecology Action won 3 awards, was taken over by the city of Palo Alto to be run as an ongoing city service.

Currently, Ecology Action consists of 3 self-supporting projects: 1) An *organic garden supply store* offering inexpensive seeds, tools, books, fertilizers and gardening advice. Store sales pay for one full-time staff person and support free weekly classes on the biodynamic/French intensive method 2) *Urban homesteading information and supplies.* Adjoining the store is a library on topics such as cheesemaking, black-smithing, raising chickens and bees, tending goats, and other skills. Ecology Action maintains files on experienced people, publishes a monthly newsletter of local information and offers periodic classes. Membership fees ($5 per year) support the library and newsletter. 3) a 3 3/4 acre *community and research garden*. A half acre is set aside for research on the biodynamic/French intensive method. 3 1/4 acres is currently available to the community. Over 300 people garden there free of charge. Currently, the research garden staff includes 4 paid staff and 7 apprentices. Salaries and stipends are paid out of sales of this book and contributions from foundations, corporations and individuals.

Ecology Action Offerings

1. A free five-week class series on the biodynamic/French intensive method on Saturday mornings.

2. Tours of the research site each Saturday at 2 pm.

3. Apprenticeships to those who are sincere, committed and responsible. The two key questions asked of interested workers are: Can you make a 1-2 year commitment? and How do you expect to be using the skills and knowledge when you leave?

4. We will answer short questions by phone or by mail if a stamped self-addressed envelope is enclosed. We continue to develop information sheets covering the commonest questions.

Our main work is the continued testing of the biodynamic/ French intensive method yields, spacings, timing, varieties, resource consumption, economic viability and sustainability. We need and welcome support for this work. You can become a garden supporter for $25 a year. This support is tax deductible.

Seeding beds using 2-inch chicken wire frames to eliminate thinning. Note flat topped beds. As soil structure improves, beds are mound shaped.

Beds are watered lightly each day. The loose rich soil makes optimum use of water and close spacing minimizes evaporation so the biodynamic/French intensive method uses one-quarter to one-thirty-first the water of standard methods.

Perhaps it is unfair to compare the yields we obtain on our hard clay sub-soil with commercial agricultural yields. Stunted broccoli plant on the left was grown using normal backyard techniques: loosening the soil and adding chemical fertilizer. Broccoli shown in the middle was obtained by loosening the soil 12 inches deep and incorporating a 3-inch layer of aged manure with some compost. Broccoli on the right demonstrates the superiority of the biodynamic/French intensive method.

Applications

The biodynamic/French intensive method, with its high yields, low water and fertilizer consumption and soil-building techniques is eminently practical for serious small-scale food production. Some possible applications are:

☐One mini-farmer may be able to net $10,000 to $20,000 a year on a 1/10 acre mini-farm. He or she would work a forty-hour week and take a 4-month vacation each year.

☐A backyard gardener in the United States could grow a year's supply of vegetables and soft fruits (322 pounds) on 100 square feet in a 6-month growing season. This food would be worth more than $150 and could eventually be grown in 5-10 minutes a day, making the gardener's time worth over $5.00/hour.

☐An entire balanced diet can possibly be grown on as little as 2,800 square feet per person in a 4-month growing season (1,400 square feet in 8 months). Using commercial agricultural techniques it takes approximately 32,300 square feet per person in India, 10,100 square feet in the United States and 4,800 square feet in Japan to grow similar diets.

☐By 1988, we hope to be producing as much food per hour by hand as commercial agriculture produces with machines.

Key points such as low start-up cost, low water usage, and diversity of crops, make the biodynamic/French intensive approach especially viable for small farmers in the developing world. This decentralized, self-sufficient approach is consistent with current emphasis on enabling poor countries to provide their own food.

Sustainability

The most important element in assessing agricultural systems is whether or not the yields are sustainable in an environmentally balanced way. For hundreds of years the Chinese practiced a manual, organic form of intensive farming using only fertilizers grown or produced on the farmstead. They were able to feed 1.5 to 2 times more people per acre than the United States presently does with mechanized chemical techniques (assuming similar non-meat diets). In addition, chemical techniques deplete the soil's capacity to produce. Wilson Clark, in the January, 1975 issue of *Smithsonian*, noted: "Even though more corn was produced per acre in 1968 than in the 1940's, the efficiency with which crops used available (nitrogen) fertilizer actually declined fivefold."

Chemical agriculture requires ever-increasing fertilizer at an increasing cost as petroleum supplies dwindle. Use of chemical fertilizers depletes beneficial microbiotic life, breaks down soil texture and adds to soil salinity. Impoverished soil makes crops more vulnerable to disease and insect attack, and requires larger energy output in the form of pesticides to sustain production. "A modern agriculture, racing one step ahead of the apocalypse, is not ecologically sane, no matter how productive, efficient, or economically sound it may seem." (John Todd in *The New Alchemy Institute Bulletin, No. 2*)

Biological agriculture can sustain yields because it puts back into the soil those elements needed to sustain fertility. A small-scale personal agriculture recycles the nutriments and humus so important to the microbiotic life forms that fix atmospheric nitrogen and produce disease-preventing antibiotics. The biodynamic/French intensive method nurtures soil life and texture, utilizes renewable resources, can be productive economically on a small manual scale, and provides higher yields.

POTENTIAL OF SMALL-SCALE BIOINTENSIVE FOOD-RAISING AS INDICATED BY ECOLOGY ACTION'S RESEARCH TO DATE

Production as compared to U.S. commercial averages, per unit area

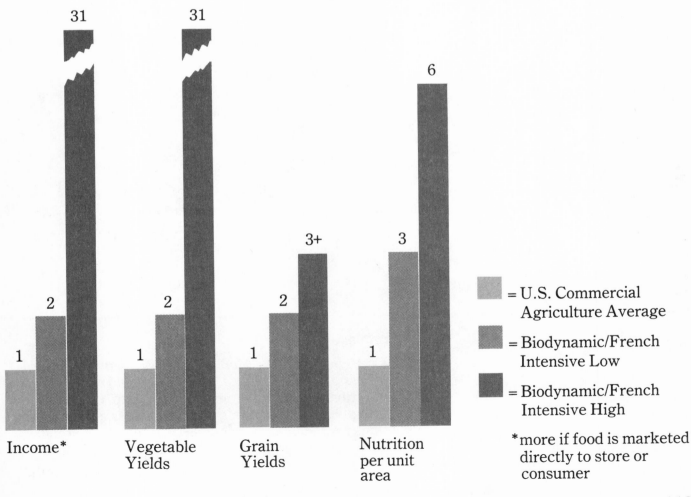

= U.S. Commercial Agriculture Average

= Biodynamic/French Intensive Low

= Biodynamic/French Intensive High

*more if food is marketed directly to store or consumer

Pounds of food produced per hour

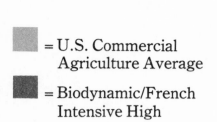

= U.S. Commercial
Agriculture Average

= Biodynamic/French
Intensive High

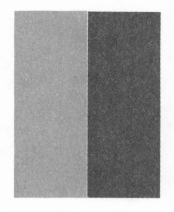

Potentially can reach the same as
with machines as soil improves,
practitioner's skills increase, as
yields increase, and through the
use of new, simple, labor saving
hand devices.

Resource use as compared with U.S. commercial average, per pound of food produced

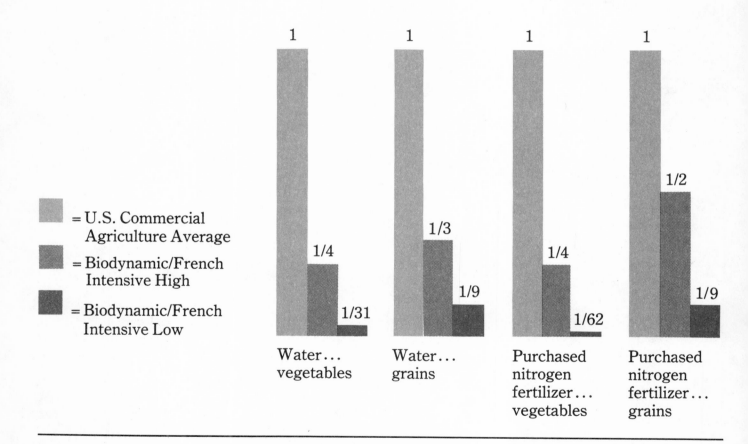

= U.S. Commercial
Agriculture Average

= Biodynamic/French
Intensive High

= Biodynamic/French
Intensive Low

Water... vegetables Water... grains Purchased nitrogen fertilizer... vegetables Purchased nitrogen fertilizer... grains

EA Publications

John Jeavons, *How To Grow More Vegetables Than You Ever
    Thought Possible On Less Land Than You Can Imagine,*
    Ecology Action of the Midpeninsula, Palo Alto, CA Revised
    1979, 128 pp. Ecology Action's popular primer giving basic
    instructions for the biodynamic/French intensive method.

John Jeavons, *1972 Preliminary Research Report,* Ecology Action
    of the Midpeninsula, 1973, 22 pp. Ecology Action's first data

report on the biodynamic/French intensive method and implications for small farmers.

1972-1975 Research Report Summary, Ecology Action of the Midpeninsula, 1976, 19 pp. Summary of data and projections of Ecology Action's first 4 years of research with intensive techniques.

Michael Shepard and John Jeavons, *Appropriate Agriculture*, Intermediate Technology, Menlo Park, CA, 1977, 14 pp. Paper given by Peter N. Gillingham at a "Small is Beautiful" conference featuring Dr. E.F. Schumacher at the University of California at Davis.

John Jeavons, "Quantitative Research on the Biodynamic/French Intensive Method", in *Small Scale Intensive Food Production— Improving the Nutrition of the Most Economically Disadvantaged Families*. Workshop proceedings prepared on behalf of the Office of Nutrition, Bureau for Technical Assistance, U.S. Agency of International Development. Published by League for International Food Education, Washington, D.C., 1977, pp. 32-38.

Bibliography for Home Gardeners, Ecology Action of the Midpeninsula, 9 pp. Well annotated basic reading list.

One-page information sheets:

Backyard Gardening—intensive techniques for home food production

Mini-Farming—brief outline of advantages and applications of Ecology Action's small-farming approach

The Herbal Lawn—step-by-step instructions on growing a self-fertilizing low maintenance lawn

Black & White Photo Set—pictorial introduction to Ecology Action's research site.

Intensive Gardening—Less Water and Higher Yields—reprint from Organic Gardening and Farming Magazine, July, 1977 July, 1977

The U-bar—a faster, easier way to prepare the soil

—Related Publications by Other Organizations—

Intensive Small Farms and the Urban Fringe, Landal Institute for Small Farm Research, Sausalito, CA 1976, 93 pp. Based in part on Ecology Action's research.

A Preliminary Assessment of the Applicability of French Intensive/ Biodynamic Gardening Techniques in Tropical Settings, Direct International Development/Direct Relief Foundation, Santa Barbara, CA 1978, 47 pp. Report from on-site visits to four intensive demonstration gardens in Central America.

Y.H. Yang, "Home Gardens as a Nutrition Intervention", *Small Scale Intensive Food Production—Improving the Nutrition of the Most Economically Disadvantaged Families,* League for International Food Education, Washington, D.C., 1977, pp. 60-80.